ROGER STAUBACH
A Special Kind of Quarterback

About the Book

Roger Staubach was called the finest college football player in America when he was quarterback for the U.S. Naval Academy team. For four years following graduation he served on active Navy duty when other outstanding players of his age were making big money in professional football. Many thought Staubach would never make it to the pros. But in this exciting biography George Sullivan tells how Staubach came back to football and spurred the Dallas Cowboys to Super Bowl achievements.

Roger Staubach
A Special Kind of Quarterback

by
George Sullivan

G. P. Putnam's Sons • **New York**

SBN: GB-399-60910-5
SBN: TR-399-20419-0
Library of Congress Catalog Card Number: 74-78901
PRINTED IN THE UNITED STATES OF AMERICA
10 up

1823526

Contents

1   Cowboy Hero   **9**

2   Boyhood of a Superstar   **15**

3   Encounter with a Bird Dog   **22**

4   Beginning of a Legend   **29**

5   "Alongside John Paul Jones"   **43**

6   On the Shelf   **56**

7   Decision   **63**

8   School Days as a Pro   **70**

9   Quarterback Carousel   **89**

10   Player of the Year   **103**

11   Super Game   **119**

12   Priorities   **134**

13   Star-Crossed Season   **143**

Index   **155**

ROGER STAUBACH
A Special Kind of Quarterback

1 Cowboy Hero

On the afternoon of January 2, 1972, a sunny Sunday, a crowd of 66,311 filled Texas Stadium in Irving, Texas, to urge on the Dallas Cowboys as they faced the San Francisco 49ers.

At stake was the championship of the National Football Conference. More important, the winning team would get to play the champion of the American Conference in that holy of holies, the Super Bowl.

The Cowboys were grim and tight-lipped. But not tense, not taut. Playing in championship games was something the team did with remarkable regularity.

But always, as the Cowboys were poised to take the final step toward pro football preeminence, they would fall flat on their faces. Their record in the five previous seasons showed that they had lost two NFL championships, two conference championships, and one Super Bowl game. If the NFL Record Manual had a category titled, "Choke-ups, Team," the Dallas Cowboys would surely be among the all-time leaders.

What made the situation all the more exasperating was the fact that the Cowboys were always *supposed* to win. Year in and year out, they ranked as the best team on paper. Unfortunately, for the Cowboys, football championships are decided on the field.

Loud cheers rang out when the Cowboy players were introduced. Indeed, these players were something to cheer about.

They had Calvin Hill and Duane Thomas as running backs, two of the best in the business, if not *the* best. Hill was big and fast, a slasher; Thomas, whom the press liked to call inscrutable, was even faster, the type of runner capable of breaking free for long yardage, and a devastating blocker.

For pass receivers, the Cowboys boasted Bob Hayes, often called the world's fastest human for his exploits as an Olympic runner. "Handle with care," said the scouting reports on Hayes. Swift and clever Lance Alworth was the other wide receiver. Veteran Mike Ditka, a strong blocker, a tough competitor, lined up at tight end.

In Bob Lilly, the Cowboys owned the best defensive tackle in pro football, but Lilly had only a slight edge over Jethro Pugh, the tackle on the other side. The linebackers—Lee Roy Jordan, Chuck Howley, and Dave Edwards—were eager, fast, and loved to hit. Herb Adderley had been All Pro so many times that they called him Mr. Cornerback. Mel Renfro, who played the other corner, had speed and agility and he hit like a linebacker.

At quarterback that afternoon was Roger Staubach, finishing out his third season in a Cowboy uniform. For the greater part of those three years, Staubach had been a backup quarterback, a benchsitter, a young man recognized by his long face and clean uniform.

Early in November, with the team on the brink of a wholesale collapse, Coach Tom Landry had made Staubach the No. 1 quarterback. Roger proved to be the catalyst the Cowboys needed. The team had not lost once since he had taken over eight games ago.

Roger had a powerful arm; he threw a "hard" ball. It whistled. "Staubach," said an assistant coach for the Cowboys, "can throw a football through a car wash and it won't get wet."

No less an authority on the art of passing than Joe Namath had lauded Staubach's skills, and Joe Willie is not one to toss compliments around indiscriminately. "Roger has one of the better arms in the game, real strong," said Namath. "He's excellent on the difficult patterns to the sidelines and throwing deep. He has more than enough zing to get the ball to the receiver on time and on target."

Roger was also known for his skill as a runner, or scrambler. He'd drop back to pass, cock his arm, pause, then suddenly he'd tuck the ball to his belly and take off, scampering up the middle or skirting an end, faking and dodging as he went, while the crowd screamed in delight. Scrambling was Roger's trademark.

Football traditionalists were appalled. They believed that the quarterback should set up in the pocket and stay there. "A scrambler has never won a championship," they kept reminding people.

But Roger Staubach was not quarterback for the Dallas Cowboys that January day because he knew how to throw the football or run with it. These are

11

necessary qualities, of course, but they are not rare ones.

"I have a lot of confidence in myself," Roger said. "Not just confidence in my ability to throw or run. I mean when I go on a football field, I believe we'll win it, somehow, some way."

This will to win, this determination, was Staubach's strong suit. Even in high school, winning had been all important to him, and later, when he quarterbacked one of the finest teams in the history of the U.S. Naval Academy, he couldn't stand the thought of losing.

Nobody had ever spent four years in the Navy, as Roger had, or taken a similar hiatus for any extended period, and come back to achieve stardom in the National Football League. Nobody else had ever come close. Roger Staubach did it because he dedicated himself to doing it. "Unrelenting"—that's a good word to use when you talk about Roger Staubach.

Honest, sincere, modest, and God-fearing are some others. And one other—tough. "You *know* Roger's tough," says linebacker Lee Roy Jordan, surely a leading authority on the subject. "You don't go running all over the place like he does if you're scared of getting your fanny bruised."

Now, as Roger began warming up on the sidelines, he recalled some of the things that Landry had told the team about the 49ers. "The 49ers were in the championship last year," Landry had said, "so their attitude is bound to be a lot different this time, a lot more confident." Landry had mentioned there was personnel improvement at two key spots. Rookie wide receiver Gene Washington gave the team an outside threat they hadn't had before, and Ted Kwalick had matured to become a tight end of All-Pro caliber.

San Francisco's passing game—the slick John Brodie throwing to Washington and Kwalick—was Landry's chief concern. "Brodie's fifteen years of experience shows in the few times he's been trapped this season—eleven times," said Landry. "That means he's reading defenses very quickly and getting rid of the ball."

But Brodie failed to perform in the way Landry and everyone else thought he would. The 49ers managed to get only one first down during the first half. In the second quarter, while in the shadow of his own goalposts, Brodie threw a screen pass, but he threw it right into the hands of George Andrie, the Cowboys' big defensive end. Andrie brought it back as far as the two-yard line. Two plays later Calvin Hill plunged into the end zone. Clark's kick made it 7–0, the score at the end of the first half.

The 49ers rebounded with a field goal in the third quarter. Then came a crucial play. Dallas had the ball, third-and-seven on their own 23-yard line. Staubach called a pass with halfback Dan Reeves as the primary receiver. Reeves was to run what the Cowboys call a "shoot" pattern, heading straight down the right sideline. Roger took the snap and pedaled back. When he saw that Reeves was covering, he went back some more.

Tackle Earl Edwards burst through, but Roger managed to slither out of his grasp. Now he was inside the 10-yard line.

Reeves, meanwhile, looked back, saw what was happening and cut to the opposite side of the field. But

13

Roger kept zigzagging, so Reeves went back to where he had been originally. Linebacker Dave Wilcox, the man assigned to cover Reeves, realizing that Roger could get long yardage up the middle if he decided to run, suddenly took off in his direction.

Roger was back of the 3-yard line when he looked downfield again, and there was Reeves all by himself and waving his arms wildly. Roger threw. Reeves made the catch and got almost to midfield before he was brought down. The Dallas fans were hoarse from screaming.

Now Roger turned to his running game, handing off time and again to Walt Garrison, who had replaced Calvin Hill. And between Garrison's slants, Roger sandwiched in quick passes to Mike Ditka. At the 3-yard line, Duane Thomas turned right end for the touchdown.

Staubach had brought the team 80 yards in 14 plays, and now they led, 14–3. The 49ers immediately launched a downfield drive, but it was halted by the Dallas defense at the 34-yard line.

After the game, Staubach talked to reporters in the Dallas locker room. Blood trickled down his left arm from a gash at the elbow, the result of being flung to the Tartan Turf several times. "They were doubling on both our wide receivers," Roger said, "and watching the tight end closely, and, at first, I didn't know where to throw."

Roger's not knowing where to throw was one of the best things to happen to the Cowboys that afternoon. In the eight times he was forced into running with the ball, he gained 55 yards, which made him the team's leading rusher for the day.

"Staubach's scrambling made the difference," said San Francisco coach Dick Nolan. "He made some key first downs for them with his ability to scramble when our guys were ready to drop him. We couldn't contain Staubach, and it really hurt because they couldn't move otherwise."

There were plenty of smiles and congratulatory slaps on the back in the Dallas locker room, but none of the frenzied excitement that teams usually wallow in following an important victory. The Cowboys had been this far before, many times.

Super Bowl. That's what the Dallas players were thinking now. Winning the Super Bowl would be worth getting excited about. And maybe this dodging, darting, scrambling, rambling quarterback was the man who could win it for them.

2 Boyhood of a Superstar

After Roger Staubach had become the Cowboys' No. 1 quarterback and began to establish his professional eminence, he told football writers of the terrible frustration he suffered while sitting on the bench and watching another quarterback run the team. "I'm a poor loser," he said. "It's difficult for me to accept failure."

From the very earliest, Roger had an instinct for

excellence. He wanted to be the best; it was as simple as that. Frequently he was. Two hundred boys took part in the local Little League baseball program. Roger had the highest batting average of them all.

"I was an only child and my parents accepted my interest in sports," Roger recalls. "They encouraged me, but they never pushed me.

"I wanted to achieve for them."

The Staubachs lived in a comfortable two-story house in suburban Silverton, just north and east of Cincinnati, a community that offered plenty of vacant lots and playgrounds. Roger was born on February 5, 1942.

Roger's mother wanted him to study piano, but she never got very far with the idea. "The music teacher," says Mrs. Staubach, "couldn't compete with the kids on the front porch."

At seven Roger was playing on a neighborhood baseball team that was co-managed by his father. Since he happened to be the smallest boy on the team, he was used to fill in wherever there was a need.

One day the team's catcher failed to show up for a game. Roger donned the oversized equipment. "He did just fine," his father said proudly.

In the Staubach home, rules were set down and they were meant to be obeyed. At times Roger, who had a rebellious streak, ran into difficulty with his parents.

One morning when he was about seven, Roger was awakened by the pounding of hammers and the rip of handsaws. Workmen had begun building a new house in the empty lot next door.

"Keep away from that new house," his father told him.

"Why?"

"Because you might get hurt."

Roger obeyed—for many weeks. One afternoon he watched as workers mixed concrete and spread it for a front walk. Late in the afternoon, after the workers had gone home, Roger found the temptation too great. *How can I get hurt?* he thought to himself. *The house is almost finished.*

He crossed over into the forbidden territory, kneeled beside the new sidewalk, and firmly pressed the palm of his right hand into the fresh concrete. It oozed up between his fingers. Then he did the same with the left.

Suddenly he heard footsteps behind him. He jerked around to see the foreman.

"Hey, kid!" the man yelled. "What are you doing? Get outta here!"

Roger leaped to his feet and scurried home. The foreman followed.

Roger was in his room when he heard the doorbell chime. His mother answered. Then he heard voices in the living room.

That night Roger was spanked. Worse, he was forbidden to use the playground across the street for two weeks. That really hurt. With the punishment went an explanation that no family could function as such without certain rules and regulations.

There were other times that Roger disobeyed and needed setting straight. Looking back, he doesn't feel that his parents were harsh. "Firm" is the word that he uses. "They were always fair and loving about it."

Roger has described his childhood as "a time of harmony and contentment," adding, "when I obeyed."

All of this isn't meant to imply that Roger was kept under a tight rein. His father, a sales representative for a shoe company, was paid on a commission basis, and so his income was not predictable. It could be more than adequate one week but barely enough to cover expenses the next. When Roger was about nine, Mrs. Staubach took a job.

This meant more duties and responsibilities for Roger. As he showed himself to be capable of shouldering additional responsibility, his parents gave him greater freedom. This was the case as he went from junior high school to high school.

The schools that Roger attended served to encourage his interest in sports. His elementary school, St. John the Evangelist in nearby Deer Park, fielded teams in baseball, basketball, and football. Roger won a place on all three.

For a time Roger's parents steered him away from football because they felt he wasn't big enough. But in the sixth grade Roger began to shoot up. The one requirement for the football team was that a boy weigh a minimum of 125 pounds, and Roger had no trouble qualifying. He liked to carry the ball, and although the coach felt that he had the makings of a quarterback, he played halfback for two seasons.

As soon as football season was over, Roger would go on to basketball and then, in the spring, baseball. The team's catcher, he hit well enough to be slotted third or fourth in the batting order.

For a high school, Roger chose Purcell, a private Catholic school for boys—not surprising since he was now very serious about his religion. It happened that Purcell was one of the four schools—Elder, Roger Bacon, and St. Xavier were the others—that made up the Greater Cincinnati League, an association of teams that offered the best high school football in southwestern Ohio. At the time that Roger enrolled, Purcell, a school of about 1,200 students, would often draw 10,000 spectators for a game.

Jim McCarthy, the head coach at Purcell, never failed to field a winning team. However, no one ever accused him of being an imaginative coach. Purcell relied upon three basic offensive plays—the left halfback ran to the left, the right halfback ran to the right, or the fullback ran up the middle. All the quarterback had to do was decide which one of the three plays to use, and then execute the handoff.

Roger was shunted from one position to another. He played end during his freshman year, then halfback and later quarterback as a sophomore. "I remember the day that they made him quarterback," his mother recalls. "He didn't like it at all; in fact, he came home crying.

"Purcell High wasn't a school where the quarterback ran with the ball, and that's what he wanted to do. But after he played for a short time, he liked it."

Roger continued to play baseball and basketball in high school. He had other interests now besides sports. Religion, for one. He made attending mass a part of his daily schedule. And he had a girlfriend, pretty, blond Marianne Hoobler, whom he had known since first grade.

By the time he was ready to enter his senior year at Purcell, Roger was a gangly 6 feet 2. The Cavalier squad that he was to quarterback that fall was, as they say, loaded with talent. The offensive line averaged 205 pounds. Of the eighteen seniors on the squad, no fewer than sixteen of them would receive offers of athletic scholarships to college.

Coach McCarthy, realizing that he had a quarterback with skill as a runner, installed a series of quarterback option plays. Rolling out to either his right or left, Roger had the choice of either carrying the ball or throwing it, depending on how the defense reacted.

He didn't throw very often. Almost every rollout became a frenzied chase, with Roger ducking, dodging, faking, and slithering through the opponents' ranks for long gains as the crowd screamed.

"Roger always killed us," says Tom Balaban, who coached football at St. Xavier. "You couldn't defense against him. When our linebackers plugged the holes, he'd pass. When they dropped off, he'd run.

"And he was some runner; in fact, I'd say that he was a better runner than passer. Remember, in his senior year he was about six feet two and packed plenty of weight, so he was powerful enough to bust tackles; plus he had good speed.

"Every time we played Purcell, they beat us soundly. I was glad when Roger graduated."

One of Roger's most daring exploits came in a game against Elder High, Purcell's arch rival. The game was deadlocked and the ball in Purcell's possession, first down on the Cavaliers' 40-yard line. "Hike right 28," Roger called, as the team huddled. The play was a sweep to the right side, with Vince Eysoldt, Purcell's big and powerful running back, to do the carrying.

As the Cavaliers broke from the huddle, Roger motioned to Eysoldt. "Don't grab for the ball, Vince," he whispered. "I'm going to keep it."

Roger barked the signals. The ball snapped into his waiting hands. The guards pulled and hurried toward the right side to lead the way, Eysoldt following. Roger faked the handoff, tucked the ball to his left hip, skirted left end, and then turning on speed streaked down the sideline into the end zone. The play proved to be the turning point in a game that Purcell won with ease.

Roger's leadership ability was evident elsewhere besides on the football field. He was elected president of the Purcell student council and later in the year reigned as the school's prom king.

Roger also played summer baseball during his high school years, and he might possibly have been skilled enough to carve out a pro career in that sport. Some of his friends did. Pete Rose, for instance. Rose, who is the same age as Roger, signed a contract with the hometown Reds right after high school graduation, and went on to become one of the National League's most consistent hitters and an All Star outfielder. Eddie Brinkman, once a teammate of Roger's, received a $65,000 bonus when he signed with Washington Senators in 1961. Now with the Detroit Tigers, Brinkman rates as one of baseball's flashiest shortstops.

Roger wound up his high school football career in brilliant fashion. He was named to the all-city all-star team and chosen as a member of the South squad in the annual North-South high school all-star football game. The contest was to be played in Canton on a field adjacent to Pro Football's Hall of Fame.

Roger started the game as a safety, and he also played flanker and halfback. By the time the South coach got around to putting him in at quarterback, the game was virtually lost, but Roger almost pulled it out of the fire. He was voted the South's Most Valuable Player.

The MVP for the winning North squad was a flashy halfback from Warren, Ohio, a young man who was to go on to an All American career at Ohio State, and later win All Pro honors with the Cleveland Browns and Miami Dolphins. One day he and Roger would meet in the Super Bowl. The player's name was Paul Warfield.

3 Encounter with a Bird Dog

After Rick Kleinfeldt, a high school running back from Cincinnati, received an appointment to the U.S. Naval Academy, his father, Richard Kleinfeldt, began to develop a deep-seated interest in the Academy's athletic affairs.

One day Kleinfeldt, who worked as a chemical equipment manufacturer's representative, called upon Academy officials. "Is there any way," Kleinfeldt asked, "in which I can contribute to the Academy football program?"

"Why not be a 'bird dog,' a scout?" he was asked. "You could keep your eyes open for football talent in the Cincinnati area."

Realizing that he lacked the skill and experience necessary to spot raw talent, Kleinfeldt enlisted the aid of a friend, sportswriter Joe Quinn. He asked Quinn to prepare a list of the best football prospects in the Ohio Valley.

When Quinn turned the names over to Kleinfeldt, he pointed out Roger's. "I think this boy is the best athlete in the area," Quinn declared. "And he's a great boy—modest, very religious, a real gentleman."

Kleinfeldt sent the list to the Naval Academy, where it crossed the desk of Assistant Coach Rick Forzano. His eyes fell on Roger's name. Forzano recalled a scouting trip he had made through southern Ohio in the spring of the previous year, and he remembered watching a Purcell baseball game in which a young man named Staubach had gotten four hits. He had discussed the boy with Coach McCarthy and recalled he had described Roger as "a fine, all-round athlete."

Forzano's next move was to call McCarthy and ask to borrow game films in which Roger played a starring role. After watching Roger run with the ball, pass it, and perform some of his wild improvisations, Forzano put in a call to Kleinfeldt. "It looks like we've got something here," Forzano said. "Stay on top of this boy."

And that's exactly what Kleinfeldt did. But it was not easy because the competition had stiffened. Roger's heroics at Purcell had attracted the attention of many other schools by this time. In fact, about twenty-five different colleges were to make him scholarship offers.

Ohio State made a very determined effort to land him. Woody Hayes, the Ohio State head coach, talked to Roger several times. "We thought a lot of Mr. Hayes," Roger's mother once recalled. "He never sent an assistant. He wouldn't give up on Roger."

Like many Catholic boys with athletic ability, Roger looked toward Notre Dame. Then he learned, to his disappointment, that Notre Dame's football scholarships had already been allotted.

Roger began making trips to many of the schools that wanted him. He visited the Ohio State campus in Columbus. Michigan invited him to Ann Arbor for a weekend. Another weekend he went to Purdue University in Lafayette, Indiana. He liked it there. He felt comfortable in Lafayette, a small town, and when he attended morning mass he noticed a large number of students there.

Roger signed a letter of intent for Purdue officials. It didn't mean that he was necessarily going to attend Purdue. It was simply meant to halt the recruiting activities of other Big Ten schools or, as Roger's father put it, "get them off his back."

All of the time Kleinfeldt was keeping busy. He had developed a deep admiration for Roger and was impressed by his commitment to Catholicism. "He had a tremendous amount of faith," said Kleinfeldt.

Kleinfeldt made arrangements to drive Roger and his parents to the Naval Academy for a weekend. The Navy coaching staff was also interested in Jerry Momfort, who had played center for Purcell. The Momforts went along in another car.

Kleinfeldt feels that the visit tipped the scales in the Naval Academy's favor. Roger had a chance to meet Head Coach Wayne Hardin and members of his staff. He spent time with several of the Academy players, including Joe Bellino, who later was to win the Heisman Trophy as the best college football player in the country.

He admired the players for their enthusiasm and dedication. They seemed to have a sense of purpose.

Roger could not put off a decision much longer. More and more he was leaning toward the Naval Academy. It seemed to present all that he was seeking: a chance to play big-time athletics and receive a first-rate education in a healthy moral environment. The Academy it would be.

Wayne Hardin, Rick Forzano, and the other Navy coaches were delighted when they received the news. But their joy proved premature.

Like anyone else, Roger had to take an entrance examination—which he failed. Roger was a good student at Purcell, maintaining a B— average. No one thought he would have any difficulty, especially since the examination stressed science and mathematics, subjects that were among his strongest. But he failed to get a passing grade in the English portion of the examination.

The news that he had flunked hit Roger like a blindside block. "What do I do now?" he kept thinking.

The Naval Academy had no intention of letting

Roger get away. The Naval Academy Foundation, a private group of Academy boosters, arranged for Roger to attend New Mexico Military Institute in Roswell, New Mexico, for a year to brush up on his studies, particularly English grammar and literature.

Roger was to learn a great deal more at NMMI than syntax and sentence structure. For one thing, he learned what it was like to be away from home, far away.

Roswell, in southeastern New Mexico, about fifty miles west of the Texas border, was wholly unlike Silverton, Ohio. There would be no winter here, but a short drive from the school was Sierra Blanca, a 12,000-foot peak that offered year-round skiing. Mostly the land was flat and green. The days were invariably sunny and hot, the nights cool. The air was dry and very clean.

NMMI calls itself the West's premier military school. Its several yellow brick Gothic buildings are scattered about a forty-acre campus. There is an emphasis on rules, regulations, and discipline at NMMI, and Roger, like other incoming cadets, had to salute all those students that outranked him and address them as "sir."

Roger was one of two quarterback candidates to report to Head Coach Bob Shaw late in the summer of 1960. Although he had just taken over the team, Coach Shaw had been around. An all-Big Ten end at Ohio State, he had gone on to a pro career with the Los Angeles Rams and later the Chicago Cardinals. He once caught five touchdown passes for the Cards, an NFL record. After his retirement as a player, Shaw spent several years as an assistant coach with the Rams, the Baltimore Colts, and the Chicago Bears.

One look at Roger and Shaw knew that he had a diamond in the rough. He could throw the ball with bullet speed, but Shaw noticed that the young man's technique was all wrong. At Purcell, Roger had done most of his throwing on rollout plays, and he had developed a tendency to throw the ball in sidearm fashion.

Shaw began teaching Roger to "come over the top" with the ball, the way a pro passer throws. "Bring the ball directly overhead," he told Roger. And he demonstrated what he wanted, cocking the ball behind the right ear, then snapping it forward. "If you don't do it like this," Shaw said, "the linemen who are rushing in can easily block the ball or tip it." Coming over the top with the ball also gave Roger a tighter spiral, enabling him to be more accurate.

Shaw also worked with Roger on his faking and ball handling. He had never had a more willing pupil. Roger not only worked tirelessly on the practice field, but at night in his room he'd drill on handoffs in front of the mirror.

When it came to leadership, Shaw didn't have to teach Roger a thing. "He's one of those young men," Shaw was to say, "who is born to lead, without fanfare or bragging."

Shaw put Roger in charge of the team on the very first day. He never had cause to regret the decision.

Roger took a generally young and inexperienced team and led it to a 9-1 record. The Broncos, as the team was nicknamed, whipped Fort Lewis A & M, 52–7; they downed Eastern Arizona Junior College, 34–13; and other scores were similar. Admittedly, the quality of competition was less than the best, but in their own class Roger and his teammates were right at the top or very close to it.

Roger was named a Junior College All American. Back at the Naval Academy, Coach Hardin was rubbing his hands together in gleeful anticipation. He and Forzano sent Roger a telegram. It read: BEFORE YOU LEAVE THE NAVAL ACADEMY, YOU WILL MAKE ALL AMERICAN AND WIN THE HEISMAN TROPHY.

"By this time," Forzano declared, "everyone *knew*."

Roger also continued to play basketball and baseball. In basketball, he was named to the all-district team.

All that stood in Roger's way now was the Naval Academy entrance examination, which he had to take again. This time it was no problem. Roger Staubach was on his way.

It has now been well over a decade since Roger attended NMMI. What are his feelings about the experience? Take a look at a copy of the current NMMI catalog. There on page 3, on the letterhead of the Dallas Cowboys Football Club, is an open letter addressed to: "A Young Man With a Goal." In the letter, Roger hails NMMI for achieving ". . . a spirit woefully missing from so many of our campuses today." He describes NMMI ". . . as one of the few remaining schools in our country geared to making a 'whole man.'"

Academy officials have the same glowing praise for Roger. What kind of student, what kind of person was he? they are frequently asked. "Outstanding . . . impeccable . . . flawless," they always answer.

4 Beginning of a Legend

Incoming students at the U.S. Naval Academy are officially designated as midshipmen fourth class, but everyone calls them plebes. "Each midshipman quickly learns during this period," says the Academy catalog, "that he is a learning subordinate. . . ."

The term "learning subordinate" really doesn't describe it. Being a plebe is a vigorous test of one's temperament and character. It's a test that Roger almost failed.

Take Induction Week. On the very first day, Roger was given a haircut, shorn of what little hair he did have, photographed, fingerprinted, and blood-typed. He was issued uniforms and given a stencil with which to mark his name and laundry number on each of his possessions. Time was found to teach the class some of the basics of marching, and they were served their first meals in Bancroft Hall.

A word about Bancroft Hall, a massive structure of gray granite that houses the midshipmen and serves as the focal point for all of their activities during their four-year stay at the Academy. The Navy calls it the largest dormitory in the world. It is something like

Macy's department store with bedrooms and big assembly halls. It contains five miles of corridors and thirty-three acres of floor space. The mess hall, where midshipmen eat family style, is so spacious that all 4,300 are able to sit down and be served at one time. Within the eight wings of Bancroft Hall are medical and dental facilities, bowling alleys, a tailor shop, soda fountain, and rifle and pistol ranges.

Throughout Induction Week, Roger was introduced to an enormous variety of rules and regulations. He was told how to make his bed and care for his room. He was instructed in how to sit, stand, walk, and even breathe. He was given a heavy manual, about the size of the Manhattan telephone directory, and told it was the most important book he would receive. It was titled: *U.S. Naval Academy Regulations.*

The list of do's and don'ts he had to memorize included these:

Don't put your hands in your pockets.

Don't lie down on your bed during the daytime.

Never appear outside your room except in complete uniform.

Do proceed and return from all formations at double-time.

Do keep your eyes straight ahead when seated in the mess hall.

Do maintain a military brace at all times in Bancroft Hall.

Do march in the center of all corridors and square all corners smartly in Bancroft Hall.

Do know the number of days until your leave, the Army-Navy football game, and graduation.

Roger also had to learn a new language. A stairway was to be known as a ladder; a wall, a bulkhead. The floor was now the deck; the ceiling, the overhead.

He wasn't warned to keep quiet; instead, he was told to "pipe down." He was never told to leave, but to "shove off"; never told to stop, but to "knock it off."

He had to memorize the words to "Anchors Aweigh" and the "Navy Blue and Gold," the Academy anthem.

When Induction Week ended, Roger began attending classes in infantry, seamanship, physical education, and the handling of firearms. His life in the real world, the civilian world, seemed far behind. He hardly had time to think of Marianne or his parents.

As the summer wore on, Roger and his classmates were taught how to fire an M-1 rifle under the supervision of Marine instructors. They learned to sail Navy yawls and cruise in small patrol boats on the Severn River.

The demands upon Roger and his spare time seemed never to end. His personal freedom was almost nil.

Most of the midshipmen were able to conform. But not Roger.

He had come from a home where he had been granted a good deal of freedom. It was a jolt to have it suddenly snatched away. In addition, he was more mature than most of his classmates. Only weeks before, the other boys had been high school students. Most had never been away from home. But Roger had spent a year at NMMI, so he was less pliable than they were, less capable of adjusting to the iron discipline a plebe must endure.

Roger could accept the need for rules and regulations

necessary to maintain order and routine. He could go along with the ribbing dished out by upperclassmen. But much of what he was supposed to do seemed pointless to him, such as keeping his shoes like a mirror and memorizing long-winded regulations word for word.

Soon Roger began to receive demerits, and with the demerits he lost the few privileges he did have. In the first six months he spent at the Naval Academy, he collected one hundred demerits.

As one could expect, he also began having problems with his studies, especially in mechanical drawing and metallurgy. "It began to look," Roger has said, "as though my stay at Annapolis was going to be a very short one."

Eventually, Roger did, to use his own phrase, "shape up." A combination of factors brought about the change. Advice he received from his parents was one important influence.

And a young instructor, not much older than Roger, talked with him at length, and pointed out the reason for the rigid disciplinary code. "These regulations are meant to teach obedience," he explained to Roger. "If military men don't learn to obey an order—whether they like it or not—we'd have chaos in the Armed Forces.

"In addition, I'm convinced that obedience is the key to a contented life."

Roger came out of the experience a better person, a more inspiring leader. "To become a leader," he says, "you first have to be willing to accept authority." The leadership qualities he acquired during his Academy years mean more to him today than the awards and trophies he won on the gridiron.

Little by little, Roger's grades improved. He stopped accumulating demerits. "Then one day," he says, "I found that I suddenly loved the place."

When Roger turned out for plebe football at Dewey Field late that summer, he could hardly believe his eyes. He was only one of more than three hundred other young men. His entire class at NMMI hadn't been so large.

Of the more than three hundred candidates, twenty-four wanted to be quarterbacks. Most fell by the wayside quickly. Within a week, the competition had narrowed down to two men—Roger and a high school quarterback from New York City named Edward "Skip" Orr. Within another week, the competition had ended. Roger was No. 1.

The chief duty of the plebe team was to provide opposition for the varsity in scrimmages. The first time the two squads met, Roger found gaping holes in the varsity defenses with his pinpoint passes.

Hardin shook his head in dismay. He ordered an all-out tackling drill for the varsity the next day. When the plebes faced the varsity team a second time, the results were no different.

This time Hardin knew what was wrong. "It's not their fault," he told an assistant. "It's that guy Staubach. He's amazing!"

First-year men were not permitted to play varsity football in 1961. The Academy plebes had their own schedule of nine games. They lost only one.

During the season, Hardin asked Plebe Coach Dick

Duden to assemble his eleven best players for a photo. "I want to hold it for three years," said Hardin. "It will help us to tell how well we've judged these kids."

As the players lined up, Staubach yelled over to Hardin. "Coach!" he shouted. "Look over here. This is next year's starting team."

Hardin couldn't help but grin. He knew Roger's claim was more than an idle boast.

The plebe year and period of intensive indoctrination ended in June, but summer is never a vacation time for Academy midshipmen. Now known as third classmen, Roger and his classmates departed for two months of training at sea aboard the USS *Forrestal,* an aircraft carrier.

It was no luxury cruise. Roger chipped peeling paint and stood deck watches. He assisted in the launch and recovery of the ship's aircraft and drew duty with the engineering staff. And he attended classes in such subjects as elementary seamanship, signaling, and the rules of the nautical road.

Roger couldn't help being awed by the size of the ship. Its flight deck was 1,020 feet in length, as long as three football fields. And Roger just happened to have brought a football with him.

Throughout the summer, he practiced throwing to anyone who would run patterns for him. He threw early in the morning, not long after daybreak. And he'd throw again in the evening. Often the session would wind up in an enthusiastic touch football game.

When Roger returned to Annapolis for the school year and his first varsity season of football, his reputation was already well established. His teammates and classmates were calling him such names as "Mr. Wizard" and "Mr. Wonderful" on the basis of his brilliance as the quarterback of the plebe team the season before. Virtually all of the midshipmen conceded the starting spot on the varsity squad to Roger.

But not Coach Hardin. While he had no doubt that his future plans would involve Staubach, for the present Hardin decided that Rom Klemick, a first classman (a senior), would be the team's signal caller.

The coach's decision was hotly debated. The Navy squad had been weakened by graduation, and many of their followers felt that only Roger's talents could save the Middies from embarrassment.

Hardin could not be pressured. He had made up his mind to bring Roger along slowly. "He'll play," Hardin said, "but I want to wait for the right moment."

Roger did get to play in the opening game of the season against Penn State, but only after the Navy squad was in rout. The final score showed Penn State the winner, 41–7. Roger quarterbacked for a few minutes toward the end, throwing only two passes, one of which was intercepted. It could not be called an auspicious debut. 1823526

Klemick was again Hardin's choice the following week, as Navy downed William and Mary, 29–16. Roger watched the entire game from the bench.

Rugged Minnesota was next. It was a long afternoon for the Middies. Big and agile Bobby Bell and Carl Eller, who bulwarked the Gopher defense, and later were to enjoy standout pro careers, blasted through time and again to pressure poor Klemick, who was lucky to escape with his life. When Klemick turned the game over to Roger, the Middies trailed, 21–0, there were only two minutes left. Minnesota didn't treat Roger any more kindly than they had Klemick, and it was another day of disappointment for him.

Cornell was the next team on Navy's schedule. Navy fans realized that if the Middies couldn't trim this Ivy League opponent, the season was going to be a disaster.

The game was part of the Family Day festivities at the Naval Academy. A partisan crowd of 23,358 turned out, the largest in the history of Memorial Stadium, and they cheered the Middies' every move.

Klemick started. Cornell wasn't able to move the ball, but neither were the Middies.

The crowd began to grow restless. Late in the first quarter, following a punt, Navy had a first down on the Cornell 39-yard line. Hardin turned to Staubach. "All right, Roger," he said. "Get in there and get us going."

Two running plays netted the Midshipmen only four yards, and for the first time in his varsity career Roger was faced with a crucial play. He handled it with the coolness of a veteran. Dropping back, he cocked his arm and fired to flanker Jim Steward for a 13-yard gain. Mixing his plays artfully, Roger then marched the Middies toward the Cornell goal, and he capped the drive himself by driving across the goal line.

Roger passed for another touchdown in the second quarter, and then, on a play that originated on Navy's 31-yard line, tucked the ball to his belly and started running. Tacklers had four chances to bring him down, but he always managed to scramble away, always, that is, until a desperate leap by a Cornell defender toppled him at the 1-yard line. On the very next play, Roger plunged over for the touchdown.

Roger played a total of twenty-three minutes that afternoon. When he trotted off the field to the cheers of the crowd, Cornell was in tatters. He had completed 9 of 11 passes for 99 yards and one touchdown, and run 89 yards and scored 2 more touchdowns on 8 carries. Navy won, 41–0. From that October day, Roger Staubach was the No. 1 quarterback at the U.S. Naval Academy.

The big test for Roger came early in December that year when the Midshipmen were to face Army's cadets. Roger was nineteen at the time, crew-cut and boyish-faced. Only a few weeks before he was unknown and virtually untried. Now he was suddenly thrust into the frenzy of the Army-Navy game as a featured performer.

This year the game was to be fought with more than the usual amount of dedication. Coach Hardin had been quoted as saying that the Midshipmen were going to beat Army, and beat them by a greater margin than they had in 1959, when the final score showed Navy on top, 43–12. Army Coach Paul Dietzel laughed off Hardin's prediction. No team in the country was capable of beating Army by that margin, Dietzel declared.

The verbal warfare was only a part of it. Navy had won three consecutive games in the rivalry, and thus Army was desperate for a victory. Because of the team's failure to handle the Middies in recent seasons, Academy officials had fired the coach and brought in the then-popular and successful Dietzel from Louisiana State University. It was Dietzel's mission to sink the Navy, and D-Day was now at hand.

There was more than the usual incentive for Hardin and the Midshipmen, too. No Navy coach had ever beaten Army in four consecutive games. Here was the opportunity to establish a record.

Navy was also out to prove that it was a better team than its disappointing 4-5 record might indicate. Under Staubach's command, however, the Midshipmen had had some fine days. They had upended a strong Pittsburgh team, and against Southern California, the No. 1 team in the nation, they had come with an eyelash of scoring a touchdown that would have earned them a tie.

Army had a better record, winning six of their first seven games, but they had lost the next two contests. So, like Navy, they were seeking to overcome a generally frustrating season. The Cadets stressed defense. The team's tough defensive unit, known as the Chinese Bandits, made few mistakes. They had limited Penn State, Pittsburgh, and Syracuse to a total of 15 points.

In the days before the game, students at both schools worked themselves into a fever pitch. Bedsheet banners were draped from dormitory windows. At Bancroft Hall, the biggest banner of all waved from above the front entrance, and it announced: HOME OF ROGER STAUBACH.

Roger was also on the mind of Army's cadets. At the Army practice field, Coach Dietzel rigged up a life-size dummy, outfitted it in cleats, football pants, and a jersey bearing Roger's No. 12. He then instructed his defensive players to tear the stand-in to shreds.

The Navy team left the Academy for Philadelphia on Friday morning, the day before the game. Following tradition, each player was carried down the steps of Bancroft Hall by clusters of midshipmen. As the buses bearing the team left the yard, the brigade followed them all the way to the gate, singing, chanting, and cheering.

Close to 100,000 people were expected to jam every corner of Philadelphia Stadium for the game. Millions more were to watch on television.

Before the game began, a brigade of 4,100 midshipmen and a corps of 2,500 cadets paraded into the stadium, and then entertained the huge throngs with songs, cheers, and stunts. The Army mules and Navy goat got into the act, and floats and the booming sound of cannons added to the hurly-burly.

President Kennedy arrived shortly before the kickoff, in time to officiate at the coin toss ceremonies. Surrounded by members of his cabinet, he would sit in the warm fall sunshine bare-headed and without a topcoat. Plans called for him to watch the game from the Navy side of the field during the first half, then cross to the Army side for the second half, so as to appear neutral. The President had quarterbacked a PT-boat as a Navy lieutenant during World War II, so, as one sportswriter remarked, "It was easy to guess which team he was neutral for."

As part of Navy's pregame high jinks, the midshipmen constructed a float on which was depicted a Chinese junk manned by a crew of Chinese bandits. A

Navy destroyer was in close pursuit. The ship's guns suddenly roared and belched red smoke, the junk crumbled and its crew fled. It was the shape of things to come.

About midway in the first quarter, Army tried a field goal and failed. The ball went over to Navy, first down on the Army 20-yard line. Staubach, a Jolly Roger emblem on his helmet glistening in the sun, swung into action. He hit end Ed Merino with a bullet pass, the play covering 39 yards. Now the Midshipmen were ignited, and they moved through the Chinese Bandit defense as no team had been able to do all season. Time and time again, Roger brought the crowd to its feet with his resourcefulness in eluding tacklers when trapped. With it third and eight on the Army 12-yard line, Staubach drilled a pass over the middle, threading it neatly between a pair of Army defenders and into the outstretched arms of end Neil Henderson. *Touchdown!* Roger had guided the Middies 80 yards in just nine plays.

The next time Navy got the ball, Roger put on a repeat performance, bringing the team 63 yards, again in 9 plays. With the ball on the Army 22-yard line, Roger setting up to pass, drifted back to the 30. He looked for a receiver; instead, he saw Army rushmen blitzing in. So he took off, circling wide, skirting left end, then cutting back to his right. He outran an Army defender at the 17 and raced right past another cadet at the 12 on his way to the end zone.

Army was never really in the running after that. The score was 15–6 in favor of Navy at the end of the second period, and 34–14 at the end.

As the gun sounded, the Navy team hoisted Hardin to their shoulders, and they marched him about the field as the band played "Navy Blue and Gold." Hardin, his face wreathed in a wide smile, gave a victory salute.

Midshipmen were pouring out of the stands and onto the field. They hurdled the low restraining barriers and headed for Roger. He had no choice but to allow himself to be picked up and hauled about. At first the surging mass of midshipmen headed for a stadium exit, as if they planned to bear Roger all the way back to Annapolis. Hardin spotted what was happening and yelled, "Bring him over here!" He pointed to a runway that led to the dressing room. Thus Roger was able to make his escape.

One account of the game called Roger the "utter ruination" of Army. Statistics bear out the statement. Roger completed 10 of 12 passes for 204 yards and 2 touchdowns. He ran for 2 other touchdowns and, in total, gained more yards than any other Navy back.

"Staubach is head and shoulders above all other quarterbacks," said Army Coach Dietzel. "He's a beautiful, unbelievable passer. He's a scrambler; he can run. It's impossible to defend against him."

Amidst the unbridled joy in the midshipmen's locker room, Roger, his grinning face showing a dab of lampblack under each eye, was the very model of Academy decorum. Reporters who clustered about him asking questions got answers like these:

"Our team was in back of me, sir."

"I had some lucky plays, sir."

"Our team had its best effort of the season, sir."

"Yes, it was a great thrill, but I'm looking forward to beating them next year."

A reporter with a tape recorder asked, "Where did you learn to pass and call plays?"

"From Bob Shaw at the New Mexico Military Institute," Roger answered.

The New Mexico Military Institute? Few people had ever heard of the place.

Roger said that he was eager to see his parents and his girlfriend, who had been in the stands. He didn't realize that his father was there, caught up in the dressing-room crush.

"It's the first time I've seen him play since high school," Mr. Staubach said. "The boy's worked for this day. All last summer, he threw the ball twice a day."

Then he added, "I'm almost too proud to talk."

It was a wild and wonderful day for Roger, one filled with unforgettable memories—the pregame spectacle, the thrill of a 65-yard scoring pass, winning, the midshipmen pouring out of the stands afterward to hoist him on their shoulders, the excitement of the locker room (which included shoving the fully clothed coaches into the showers), and, the next day, the return to Annapolis where the midshipmen turned out in special formation for the ringing of the victory bell.

There would be other Army-Navy games for Roger, and he would lead a winning Navy team again. But there would never be another game like this. When the teams met the following year, President Kennedy was dead fifteen days and the afternoon was darkened by his murder. The next year, 1964, the game would be overshadowed by the nation's increasing involvement in Vietnam. By the 1970's, tickets for the contest were going unsold. It seems doubtful whether the contest will ever regain the popularity and public esteem it had that magic afternoon in 1962. Ask Roger Staubach to name his most vivid memories. That game is one of them.

5 "Alongside John Paul Jones"

When the football season was over and tumult had died down, Roger decided not to go out for basketball. He planned to concentrate on his studies.

The basketball team had problems from the beginning, however, and Coach Ben Carnevale put out a call for fresh playing talent. Roger was one of those who answered.

He was limited in what he could do. Because he hadn't been involved in daily practice sessions, he lacked stamina, and it would be weeks before he would begin to be consistent with his outside shots. Yet Carnevale knew that Roger could still make an important contribution.

In the final game of the season, Navy faced a heavily favored Army team. So sure was Army of winning that General William Westmoreland, superintendent of the Military Academy, attended the game, and he invited several Pentagon officials to join with him in celebrating Army's prospective moment of triumph.

When the starting lineups were introduced, Roger's name was greeted by loud cheers and stamping feet. Could the Middies' marvelous Army-killer work his magic again?

Roger was given the assignment of guarding Joe Kosciusko, the key man in Army's attack. Navy used a full court press, and Roger would pick up Kosciusko at the Army end of the court and cover him like a coat of paint.

Unable to pass or shoot in their accustomed manner, Army's best team in years foundered. Navy won, 55–48. Although Roger did not score, he was hailed as the team's hero.

After the game, a disgruntled General Westmoreland spoke to Coach Carnevale. "Why did you use Staubach? " Westmoreland asked. "He's no basketball player."

Carnevale grinned. "He may not be a basketball player," Carnevale replied, "but he's a winner."

Not long before the 1963 football season opened, Navy Coach Wayne Hardin declared, "Roger Staubach is destined to become the greatest quarterback who ever played for the Naval Academy." Hardin wasn't the only booster that Roger had, not by any means. A New York sportswriter, surveying Navy's football prospects for the year ahead, listed the team's chief assets as: "Staubach, Roger Staubach, and quarterback Roger Staubach."

Staubach wasted no time demonstrating that the appraisals were accurate. In the opening game of the season against a well-regarded Virginia team, he completed 17 of 22 passes for 171 yards. Navy won, 51–7. "We contained their running game all right," said West Virginia Coach Gene Corum, "but, of course, that made it impossible to stop Staubach's passes."

Against William and Mary the following week, Staubach was even more sensational. He picked the defense apart, completing 12 of 17 passes for 206 yards. When the linemen charged, he scrambled left or right. And when they held their ground, Roger would frequently pick out a hole and run. Navy was on top again, 28–0.

"When Roger gets that ball," said one of Navy's assistant coaches, "nobody knows what he's going to do with it except Roger and God." The Michigan game that season was a case in point. Roger had steered the team to a 14–0 lead with a minute to play in the first half. It was Navy's ball on their own 46-yard line. Staubach ran a quarterback sneak that earned a yard or so. It appeared as if he were content with the lead and running out the clock.

Now there were only six seconds left. Suddenly Roger darted back, cocked his arm, and lofted a 54-yard scoring pass to John Sai. Navy went off the field at halftime with a 21–0 lead. The play later was called the "Transcontinental Pass."

The Michigan game was Roger's best from a statistical standpoint. He connected on 14 of 16 passes for 237 yards and one touchdown, and he sprinted for 70 yards and another touchdown. "He's a great football player," said Michigan Coach Bump Elliot. "I don't know when I've seen a better one."

45

There were times, however, when he scared his own coach half to death. In the game against Michigan, Navy had the ball on the Michigan 20-yard line. Roger took the snap and rolled to his right, looking for a receiver as he ran. When Michigan's rushmen hemmed him in, Roger retreated. He kept going back, his pursuers lunging at him as he went. Finally, at midfield, they surrounded him and closed in for the kill.

As Roger was going down, he managed to get the ball away. Somehow it ended up in the hands of Pat Donnelly and the play netted the Middies a 1-yard gain.

When Roger came off the field, Hardin was waiting for him at the sidelines. "Did you see Donnelly," the coach asked, "or were you just throwing it away?"

Roger smiled. "Let's just call it my Hail Mary play," he said.

Roger put on another frenzied performance the next week against SMU in the Cotton Bowl. The Mustangs led, 26–25, late in the final quarter. Roger guided the Middies downfield to the SMU 2-yard line. A field goal boosted them into the lead, 28–26.

But in less than a minute, SMU scored another touchdown. Passing and scrambling, Roger guided the Middies to the SMU 28-yard line. Less than a minute remained.

Once more Roger carried the ball, churning his way to the 8-yard line, where he was leveled by a cluster of SMU tacklers. Roger was slow getting to his feet. His head buzzed.

Time for one last play, he knew. He called a pass with Skip Orr to be the primary receiver. As Roger set up to throw, he saw Orr cross the goal line and make his cut. Roger threw. The pass was high. Orr made a desperate leap. Roger watched as the ball grazed Orr's fingertips and fell to the ground. The gun sounded ending the game. Navy had lost.

The Middies bounced back to beat Virginia Military Institute and Pittsburgh. Notre Dame was next. Coach Kuharich had reason to lament his school's lukewarm attitude toward Roger when he was seeking a scholarship. He passed for 2 touchdowns in Navy's 35–14 victory.

Roger was becoming well known. Newspaper accounts of Navy's victories hailed him not only for his skill as a passer and signal caller, but for the excitement he generated with his running.

Fan mail for Roger began to pour in to the Academy, between two hundred and three hundred letters a week. The Navy furnished him with a secretary. But Roger made it plain that he wanted to be consulted concerning each reply. "When a kid writes," he said, "you can't just say, 'Hi.'"

Back in Cincinnati, Roger's parents kept a scrapbook containing news clippings about their son's career. They found him reluctant to talk about his achievements.

"I've talked to him every week after the game," Roger's father said, "but, from the conversation, you wouldn't know that he played football. And all he says in his letters is, 'I hope we win next week.'"

Marianne Hoobler plastered the wall of her bedroom with pictures of Roger. The couple were "engaged to be engaged" now, and Marianne wore Roger's high school ring and midshipman pin. "They think a great deal of each other," said Roger's mother, a remark notable for its understatement.

After the Middies whipped Maryland, Roger's name appeared as the quarterback on a major All America team. His teammates kidded him about it. "Speech! Speech!" they demanded one day after a practice session.

Roger got up on a bench. His teammates were expecting humility. Fighting to keep a straight face, Roger began, "This has been a terrific year . . . but if only I could have gotten a little blocking."

Duke fell next, giving the Middies an 8–1 record. Only Army remained on Navy's schedule.

Roger's smiling face was featured on the cover of *Time* magazine, and the article inside called him "easily the most electrifying player in a college uniform," and lauded him for his "magnificent magic."

The honors rolled in. The Associated Press and United Press International named him "Back of the Year." To *Sport* magazine, Roger was "Top Performer in College Football." Every major All America team sported his name.

Army's football team was not impressed. While the Middies managed to beat the Cadets, 21–15, the game easily could have gone the other way. Army had the ball on Navy's 2-yard line when time ran out.

Navy wound up the season with a 9-1 record, ranking as the nation's No. 2 team. As for Roger, he ended the season with 107 completions in 161 attempts, a 66.4 percentage. His passes earned 7 touchdowns and 1,474 yards. He rushed for 418 yards and another 8 touchdowns. He also caught 3 passes for 35 yards.

Roger won the Heisman Trophy last year, and he won it in a landslide. He was the No. 1 choice in 517 of 784 ballots. Billy Lothridge, a quarterback at Georgia Tech, second in the balloting, captured 65 first-place votes. Roger's "victory" marked only the fourth time in the 29-year history of the Heisman that a junior had won it.

There were many other fine college quarterbacks that season. Besides Billy Lothridge at Georgia Tech, who not only passed and ran with the ball, but punted and placekicked, there was Alabama's Joe Namath, whose deadly passing had gotten Alabama into the Orange Bowl. Southern California had Pete Beathard. His rifle arm and skill in running option plays had pro scouts falling over one another. Miami boasted George Mira, rated college football's best pure passer.

Newsweek magazine called it "The Year of the Quarterback," then added that Roger Staubach was "Quarterback of the Year."

Roger was invited to New York to accept the Heisman Trophy at a dinner at the Downtown Athletic Club. Before the presentation, Roger's father was invited to speak.

"I'll make it short," Mr. Staubach began. "We had only one child. The good Lord gave us a good one."

For the Midshipmen that year, the season had a postscript to it. Not long after the team had beaten Duke, Navy was invited to the Cotton Bowl. "We'll accept," said Academy officials, "if we beat Army." And then they had beaten Army.

The game shaped up as a major showdown, in that

49

the Middies, the country's No. 2 team, were to face Texas, the team ranked No. 1. It was to be a fitting climax to one of the most exciting college seasons in years.

The Longhorns, the only major college team with a perfect record, played tough ball-control football, relying on a grinding running game and a rock-ribbed defense bulwarked by Scott Appleton, the most widely hailed college lineman of the year. Texas had not yielded more than 13 points in any game that season. Darrell Royal, their coach, was one of the best in the business.

Texas undoubtedly would have been favored were it not for Roger. "Staubach's presence," said the New York *Times,* "gives Navy virtually an even chance of beating Texas because of his ingenious resourcefulness, and his talents as a passer, runner, and field general." The *Times* also hailed halfback Johnny Sai for his breakaway speed, and fullback Pat Donnelly for his driving power. But it was Roger with his "unsurpassed skill and poise," said the *Times,* that made the match an even one.

The Longhorns had devised a simple method of stopping Roger's scrambles. They assigned Scott Appleton to watch him carefully. Whenever Roger lurched to the right, Appleton was to go to the left— and wait for him to come by.

The Cotton Bowl had been sold out to its capacity of 75,540 for weeks. Among those who watched were Paul H. Nitze, Secretary of the Navy, and Admiral David L. McDonald, Chief of Naval Operations. A contingent of five hundred Academy midshipmen had been flown down from Annapolis. Millions upon millions tuned in on television.

The weather was perfect, sunny and mild. Navy kicked off. Within minutes Texas had crossed into the Navy end zone for the game's first touchdown.

After the kickoff, Roger led his teammates out onto the field—to a mugging. The Longhorns began by shutting off Navy's running game, just as surely as you shut off a faucet. The Middies found it impossible to open holes in the Texas line, and when they tried to sweep, the Texas linebackers poured through to rack up the runner before he could even make the turn. For the game, Navy was to show a minus 14 yards rushing.

Roger's only hope was to pass. The first time he tried, Texas defenders had him in their grasp before he had a chance to look for a receiver. He managed to squirm free but to no avail; he was tackled for a 22-yard loss. Time and time again, he was thrown for losses throughout the first half.

The Texas quarterback, Duke Carlisle (who had scarcely been heard of before the game and never has been since) had an easy time of it. The first Longhorn touchdown came as a result of one of his passes, and in the second quarter he threw for another, the play covering 63 yards.

Not long after the second Texas touchdown, Roger suffered his harshest indignity in a long afternoon of indignities. Scampering back to pass, he was hit so hard that the ball popped out of his hands. Texas' Bobby Gramblin recovered on the Navy 34-yard line.

Six plays later the Longhorns scored their third touchdown.

What is important about the game is the way Roger reacted. Though "harried unmercifully" (as one account of the game put it), and though he was being hit harder than he had ever been hit before (as he was to tell the press after the game), Roger would not let himself be intimidated. Indeed, he fought back. Late in the third period he led the team on its first sustained drive of the game. With the five hundred midshipmen on their feet and screaming, Roger completed pass after pass to Skip Orr and Pat Donnelly. The drive covered 67 yards, but the half ended before Roger could get the ball across the goal.

Texas scored a fourth touchdown late in the third quarter, and the outcome was never in doubt after that. Roger's passes brought the Middies 75 yards in the final quarter, the drive ending when Roger, darting back to pass, was unable to find a receiver, so he sprinted to his right for three yards and a touchdown. The try for a 2-point conversion failed. The final score: Texas, 28; Navy, 6.

What had happened? Simple. Rear Admiral C. C. Kirkpatrick, the superintendent of the Naval Academy, said it best: "They beat the hell out of us."

There could be no doubt about it—the Texans were a vastly superior force. They blitzed and harried Roger throughout the afternoon. They pounded him to the ground so many times he lost count. Yet Roger remained cool. In accounts of the game, it is often overlooked that he set a Cotton Bowl passing record that afternoon, completing 21 of his throws for 228 yards.

After the game, Roger sat in front of his locker stall and tried to explain to reporters how he felt.

"It's the worst feeling you can ever have," he said. "I felt good at times. I felt confident. I felt I could run. I felt I could pass.

"But something always happened. There were no openings, or if there were any I couldn't find them.

"I've got another year, thank God. I'd hate to have it all end like this."

In the weeks that followed, Roger learned to joke about the setback. Not long after the game, he attended a dinner in Philadelphia where he was to be presented with the Maxwell Trophy, given annually to the outstanding college player by the Maxwell Memorial Football Club of Philadelphia. When Roger was introduced, the master of ceremonies, referring to his tendency to scramble, said, "Only God and Roger Staubach know what he's doing out there."

After the introduction, Roger went to the microphone. "I want to make a slight change in what was said," he declared. "Only God, Roger Staubach, and *Scott Appleton of Texas* know what he's doing out there."

What happened in the Cotton Bowl on New Year's Day, 1964, signaled the beginning of a grim period in Roger's football career. In the opening game of his senior season in the fall, he tore muscles in his leg and pulled tendons in his foot. He missed the next game entirely and played only a few minutes of each one of the next three contests.

He eventually recovered, completely, and in the last

three games of the season before the clash with Army—against Notre Dame, Maryland, and Duke—Roger gained 701 yards with his passing and running.

Still, it was not a successful season, with the team showing a 3-5-1 record as the meeting with Army drew near. The Cadets then managed further to blacken the year by trimming Roger and his teammates, 11–8.

As a student, Roger was earnest and diligent. "He has to work for everything he gets," said one instructor. The course of study at the Academy was not exactly reading, 'riting, and 'rithmetic. It included such subjects as differential equations, electrical science, thermodynamics, and computer science. In his senior year, Roger carried a C average and ranked six hundred and twentieth in a class of nine hundred and five.

The Academy also rates midshipmen on their military aptitude and leadership qualities. In this regard, Roger wasn't far from the top—twelfth in the class.

"When you talk of Navy legends, Roger Staubach ranks right alongside John Paul Jones." That was the way a press release from the Naval Academy summed up Roger's career.

During May of his final year, Roger learned that he had been named to receive the Academy's two most coveted awards—the Thompson Trophy and the Naval Academy Association Sword. Roger was only the fourth midshipman in sixty-five years to win both prizes.

It marked the third consecutive year that Roger had taken the Thompson Cup, given to the midshipman "who has done the most during the current year for the promotion of athletics at the Naval Academy."

The sword is presented to the graduating midshipman who is considered "to have personally excelled in athletics" during his years of varsity competition.

The day before he graduated, Roger was paid the ultimate compliment. His famed No. 12 was retired to the Academy trophy case, only the second time in history that that had happened. Joe Bellino's No. 27 had been similarly retired.

Roger practically rewrote the Academy football record book, owning or sharing eight all-time records. He gained a total of 4,253 yards running and passing in his three-year varsity career, more than any other player since 1879, the year that the Academy began keeping records. Roger completed a splendid 63.1 percent of his passes—292 of 463—still (through 1972) an NCAA record.

Football, of course, wasn't Roger's only sport. He lettered in basketball during his sophomore year, and he won three Navy monograms for baseball. He posted a batting average of just over .300 and captained the team as a senior.

Roger's greatest fans were within the Academy. His classmates and other midshipmen often sought his picture and asked him for his autograph. The fact that he was deeply religious was well known. When he was graduating, the company that he was attached to wanted to give him a gift, something personal, something they knew he would like. After taking up a collection, they bought him a pair of rosary beads.

More than once in that final year at Annapolis, Roger had thought of what it would be like to play professional football. This was the period that the

NFL and the upstart American Football League were involved in a hot war for playing talent, and players' salaries were skyrocketing. Roger was stunned by some of the sums being handed out.

Roger frequently watched the pro games on television. *Heck, why couldn't I do just as well?* he thought to himself.

But he knew that he "owed" the Navy four years of service. It was an obligation he meant to fulfill.

Roger could easily have wriggled out of his commitment with the Navy. It happens all the time. He could have flunked a course. He could have gotten married as an undergraduate. Or, on the basis of some football injury, he could have applied for and probably been granted a medical discharge.

But doing any one of these things would have been as alien to Roger as selling military secrets to the North Vietnamese. He had pledged himself to serve four years, and so he would.

6 On the Shelf

Roger's 1965 football season was brief—one game. As Ensign Rogert T. Staubach, he reported to Evanston, Illinois, in mid-July for the College All Star Game. The collegians were to face the pro champion Cleveland Browns in the annual charity game at Soldier Field sponsored by the Chicago *Tribune*.

At the Evanston training camp, Roger met quarterback John Huarte from Notre Dame, who had won the Heisman Trophy the previous season and then signed for the New York Jets for something more than $200,000. But that was only pocket money compared to what a quarterback named Joe Namath was going to be paid. The talk was that the former Alabama star was going to receive more than $400,000 in bonus money from the Jets.

Craig Morton, fresh from the campus of the University of California, was another quarterback at the All Star camp. At 6 feet 4, taller than Roger by a full inch, and outweighing him by fifteen pounds, Morton had been drafted by the Dallas Cowboys, and once the All Star game was out of the way he would be heading for the Cowboy training camp.

Roger's teammates may all have been much wealthier than he was, but it was he who impressed the squad the most. "After thirty minutes on the field," said tackle Ralph Neely of Oklahoma, "we could have taken a vote and elected Staubach captain.

"I don't know why—it's just something about the guy that exudes leadership. He's got it."

Neely's evaluation was confirmed a few days later when the squad did vote Roger to be a team captain. He worked diligently preparing for the game. There was a possibility, he realized, that it might be the last game he'd ever play.

Roger earned a starting assignment, although he has joked he might not have won it on merit. The All Star coach was Otto Graham, and Graham, Roger points out, just happened to be a captain in the Naval Reserve.

Played at night on a wet and sloppy field, the game

was a bad one for Roger. He had a tendency to jump into the air when throwing swing passes, and once when he did this, Galen Fiss, a blitzing linebacker, roared in and smashed Roger to the ground. Roger felt a stab of pain and grabbed for his shoulder. They helped him from the field and sat him on the bench. As he stared at the ground, his shoulder throbbing with pain, he heard the public address announcer say, "Craig Morton now at quarterback for the All Stars."

Roger played no more that night. He had dislocated his shoulder.

On September 4, 1965, Roger and Marianne were married in St. Peter in Chains Cathedral in Cincinnati. They honeymooned briefly in Washington, D.C.

That fall Roger was stationed at Annapolis, where he helped to coach the Navy team. His shoulder still pained him whenever he tried throwing the ball, but it was improving steadily.

While Roger was at Annapolis, Lamar Hunt, one of the founders of the American Football League and also the owner of the Kansas City Chiefs, called Roger and asked whether he could drop by for a chat. Hunt impressed Roger with his sincerity and also with a contract offer he made. It stated that the Chiefs would guarantee Roger a generous bonus if and when he decided to leave the service.

Not long after, Roger was also contacted by the Dallas Cowboys. Both teams had previously drafted Roger.

Roger decided to turn the negotiations over to a close friend, one Paul Borden, a career Navy man, a captain, and also a lawyer. Borden told the Cowboys that Roger had no intention of putting himself on the auction block. The Cowboys, said Borden, could make one offer. If it was better than the Chiefs' offer, then Roger would sign with the Cowboys. If it wasn't, then Roger would join the Chiefs. But there was to be one offer and only one from each team.

The Cowboy contract that Roger ultimately signed was not the standard NFL agreement. It had a couple of unusual features. First, it provided that Roger was to be paid a bonus just for signing (said to be $50,000). Second, it gave Roger the option of staying in the service. If that was to be his choice, and he never played a pro game in his life, he was still to receive the bonus and the modest salary for which the contract also provided.

Roger was undecided at this time whether to make the Navy his lifetime career or give pro football a try. After all, there was no need to make the decision for another four years. But he now knew that if he were to choose the pro game, he at least had a goal, a target at which to shoot. The contract assured him of that.

In December that year, Roger enrolled as a student at the Navy supply school in Athens, Georgia. It was his last stopover before he was sent to Vietnam.

Although going to Vietnam meant that Roger and the now-pregnant Marianne would be apart for the first time, they were resigned to the assignment. They realized, for a Naval officer, at least, being shipped to Vietnam in 1966 was just about as much a part of service life as having shined shoes.

Roger arrived at Da Nang, the huge air base on the

east coast of Vietnam south of Hue, in August, to be led to a tiny office in the corner of an enormous warehouse. This was to be Roger's headquarters for the next few months.

At the time of Roger's arrival in Vietnam, the American buildup was in full sway. There were about 245,000 troops there, and the number would more than double in the next eighteen months. Public opinion in opposition to the long and divisive conflict was just beginning to develop.

With men, supplies and equipment flooding in from the United States, Roger, as a supply officer, seldom had a free moment. But most of what leisure time he did have he devoted to football. It happened that Steve Roesinger, a classmate of Roger's at the Naval Academy, and a substitute end on the football team, was also stationed at Da Nang. After dinner each evening, Roger threw passes to Roesinger on a Vietnamese soccer field.

Roger practiced throwing more to keep in shape than anything else, for he was still dubious about a career in pro football. "I only know that I'm going to stay in condition and make the decision when the time comes," he told the Associated Press not long after he had arrived in Vietnam. "Even if I stay in the Navy, which is certainly possible, I want to stay in good shape."

When August melted into September, Roger began to listen to play-by-play broadcasts of games on the Armed Forces Radio Network, and he read all that he could about the game in whatever news magazines he was able to get his hands on. He found that he missed the game much more than he had ever expected he would, and throwing passes to Steve Roesinger was no substitute for competition.

As much as he missed sports, Roger missed his family more. Now, besides Marianne, there was Jennifer, who had been born in June, two months before Roger had been sent overseas. Marianne's frequent letters brought Roger news about his infant daughter, but he longed to be with them.

In January, 1967, when the Green Bay Packers played the Cowboys for the NFL championship, Roger listened in on radio. With sixteen seconds remaining, Green Bay quarterback Bart Starr tucked the ball to his chest and knifed his way across the Dallas goal line for the winning touchdown.

Very soon after the game, Roger sat down and wrote a letter to Gil Brandt, a Dallas official and now the club's vice-president in charge of personnel development. In part, it said:

DEAR GIL:

Just a short note to let you and the Dallas people know that I followed the team as closely as I possibly could this year. I was very proud to say that I was just a small part of the Dallas football organization.

I listened to the championship game on a playback on Armed Forces Radio. It was a pretty fantastic game and I know it was quite a disappointment to the team after coming so far the whole season. I would have given anything to have seen the game especially the final quarter when Dallas was on the two-yard line. I tried to push them in on radio.

I'll be changing jobs this week and moving to Chu Lai. I've had the chance to take over the pier operation there. I'll have 120 enlisted men working for me and two ensigns. Should be a big job but interesting.

I've been able to throw quite a bit with a former end at the Naval Academy. We work out during dinner and have kept my arm in a ready state. Also have been able to do some isometrics. Meredith had quite a year but I hope to be ready just in case. Sure miss the game.

The football I took with me has just about had it, and if possible I would like to buy an official ball from you. It's better working with the right size. I hate to ask you for anything since it's a bother, but would appreciate your help.

Sincerely,
ROGER STAUBACH

Naturally, Brandt sent the football (without charge) and, later in the year, a film featuring highlights of Dallas games that Roger had also requested.

Roger was promoted to lieutenant, junior grade, not long before he was transferred to Chu Lai. He has described his job there as being "important," but he is quick to declare that "It wasn't anything like the guys in the field. Every one of them deserved a medal."

Roger's experience in Vietnam was not without its tragic overtones. A friend of his, Mike Grammer, who played guard on the 1963 Navy team, was found trussed up and shot to death, along with a Marine adviser. Tom Holden, another guard on the same team, was shot and killed while leading his platoon. "I believe," says Roger, "that God will be just with such men and they'll find a better life, or their deaths would be so insignificant."

Roger himself had a close call one night when the Vietcong infiltrated an offshore island and sent up a mortar barrage that killed one man and wounded three. One of the mortar shells exploded about two hundred yards away from the bunker in which Roger had taken refuge.

Roger left Vietnam in August, 1967. He wasn't sorry to go, but, as he has said many times since, "I'm glad I had the opportunity to serve there."

Roger was lean and trim when he stepped off the plane in California, about five pounds below his playing weight at the Naval Academy. He still spoke in a soft and serious manner. His hair was still crew cut. But the Vietnam experience and being away from those he loved had matured him, and his face had lost its boyishness.

7 Decision

After his return to the United States, Roger was assigned to the Pensacola Naval Air Station at Pensacola, Florida, where again his duties and responsibilities were to be those of a supply officer. Before reporting to the "Annapolis of the Air," as Pensacola is sometimes called, Roger was given permission to stop off at the training camp of the Cowboys at Thousand Oaks, California.

There he threw a few passes and chatted with some of the coaches and players, but his appearance caused little comment. Before he left, Roger was given a Cowboy playbook to study.

It was a hectic time for Roger. He was eager to collect his family and get settled at Pensacola.

He also looked forward to joining the Pensacola Goshawks, the base football team, which had already begun practicing for the upcoming season. The Goshawks played teams from the Gulf States Conference, teams such as McNeese State College, Southeastern Louisiana, and Middle Tennessee State.

At the first practice session, Roger noticed that most of the players were not as big as his teammates at Navy and they didn't compare at all in size with the Dallas Cowboys. The biggest man on the Goshawks squad weighed 225. Mike Repp, one of the team's running backs, was 5 feet 6, 150 pounds. No one kidded Mike about his size, or lack of it, however. It also happened that he was Marine Corps captain.

The Goshawks used a simple offensive system, relying on only a handful of plays. They had no other choice. Because of transfers and discharges, the team suffered a constant turnover in personnel, so the offense had to be simple enough so that a new arrival could learn the system in just a few practice sessions.

Roger found these shortcomings very easy to overlook. Just being back on a football field and having a chance to lead a team again was exhilarating. Thanks to exercise programs and all the throwing he had done in Vietnam, his arm was stronger than it had ever been, even going back to his best days at the Naval Academy. He felt sharp. He felt confident. He now began to think more seriously about a career in pro football.

What Roger did at Pensacola was just what he had done at the Naval Academy, at NMMI, and in high school—make his team win. In the season before Roger's arrival, the Goshawks had managed to win only three times in nine tries. In 1967, with Roger at quarterback, they won twice as many games, and the next year they did even better.

Roger had three skilled receivers to throw to in 1968 —Steve Dundas, an NAIA All-American at Pomona (California) College; Gary Simpson, who had experience with the Des Moines Warriors, a farm team of the Minnesota Vikings; and Tom McCracken, a Goshawk veteran. Roger's protection was also improved, although the defensemen still lacked size.

The Goshawks won four straight and then faced Youngstown State University. Roger had an incredible day. In the first half he threw for 333 yards, and for the game, in which he played less than three full quarters, he totaled 452 yards passing, more than any other game in his life. Oh, yes, the Goshawks won—58–38.

Roger's final appearance at Kane Field, the Goshawks' home base, gave evidence that he still hadn't forgotten how to run with the ball. The Goshawks were playing Bradley. On a fourth-down situation late in the game, Roger took the snap and rolled out to his left looking for a receiver, then suddenly darted back toward the middle. Vaulting over fallen players he broke downfield; he started running for the end zone 67 yards away. Not a hand touched him. When Roger came off the field, the crowd of 4,500 gave him a standing ovation.

The Goshawks won that game, 35–0, and 6 others, giving the team a 7–2 record for the season. In summing up the season, Goshawk Coach Bob Elzey paid tribute to Roger, saying that it had been "a great privilege" just to be associated with him.

"We know," said Elzey, "that he can do the job with the pros."

By this time, Roger knew it too.

It is generally agreed that the Cowboys' training camp at Thousand Oaks, California, is one of the best in the National Football League. Located about forty miles north of Los Angeles on the campus of California Lutheran College, it has all the usual facilities—dorms, meeting rooms, a practice field, etc.—but it also happens to be blessed with a weather system that approaches the ideal.

Days are sun-filled and warm, but every evening a cool breeze sluices in from the ocean. Players must wear sweaters if they're going out.

The dorm is a two-story H-shaped structure. Veterans are berthed on the ground floor of one wing, rookies on the second floor. The other wing contains coaches, club officials, and the press.

In the summer of 1968, Roger took a two-week leave from his duties at Pensacola to attend the Cowboys' training camp at Thousand Oaks. It was time to make a decision. He liked the Navy. Marianne liked being a Naval officer's wife. But the lure of professional football had become strong. He knew that if he didn't make the attempt to play pro ball, he would spend the rest of his life wondering if he should have.

When he arrived at camp and looked about him, he could not help but be impressed. There was Don Meredith, who was now being rated as one of the best four or five quarterbacks in the pro game. Although he had suffered painful injuries the season before, he had never lost his poise. Popular with his teammates, Meredith was a splendid leader, an intelligent play-caller.

Craig Morton, whom Roger remembered from All Star camp three years before, was the No. 2 quarterback. He had shown many times that he was a quality player. And behind Morton was Jerry Rhome, who had been with the Cowboys three years following a glittering career at SMU.

Obviously, the Cowboys didn't need another quarterback. But Roger didn't let the competition upset him. He wasn't there to try to take anyone's job away, merely to see what he could do.

The team had superb receivers in Bob Hayes, Lance Rentzel, and Pettis Norman, and their No. 1 draft choice that year was a young pass catcher from Alabama named Dennis Homan. To coach their receivers, the Cowboys had just hired Ray Berry, who had recently retired as an end for the Baltimore Colts, where he had established a helmetful of records of receiving.

Little by little, Roger began to realize that most of these players were fighting for jobs, just as he would be one day. He stopped looking at them in awe. He began to feel like a member of the team.

Just as important, he soon found out that he was the physical equal of these men. "I was in excellent shape," he was to say later. "I felt it was just a matter of learning and getting some experience."

It was Coach Tom Landry who impressed Roger the most. Landry's knowledge of the game was awesome, and the offensive strategy he had devised for the Cowboys reflected that awesomeness. Most teams were running plays from a basic T formation, but Landry switched his backs and receivers in double-wing, triple-wing, or slot formations, and ran a variety of plays from each.

As a player, a defensive back for the New York Giants, Landry had not been noted for his speed or quickness. But he learned to compensate by training himself to recognize the tendencies of opposition players, and to "key," to determine the flow or movement of play, by watching the moves of the opposition.

If there was any criticism of Landry, it was that he did not motivate his men. It was said that he considered the game a business and the players businessmen, guys hired to do a job. "A coach has to prepare the team technically and physically," Landry had said. "But they have to be able to motivate themselves." Landry's loudest critics called him dour and bleak, but no one ever questioned his knowledge of the game.

The first day that the veteran players checked in, Landry held a team meeting, and as the men sat quietly, he spoke to them about the Cowboys, about the team's philosophy of offense and defense. He spoke openly and confidently, and it was obvious to Roger that this man knew more about the game than he himself did. It was like sitting in a classroom at Annapolis and listening to an erudite and articulate professor explain basic Russian. Landry still impresses Roger, but in 1968 he was, to use his own term, "awe-struck" by the man.

Roger was to be tested in an intrasquad session against the Los Angeles Ram rookies. The Rams were coached by George Allen at the time. To Allen, a rookie was (and is) simply a player who can be traded for a veteran. So Roger wasn't thrown in against potential first-year players, but against experienced men and taxi-squad personnel.

As the drill was set up, Dallas was to be the offensive team for the afternoon; the Rams would provide the defense. There were to be no kickoffs and no punts. Instead, the Cowboys were to be given 11 first-down possessions on their own 30-yard line. Each time, they would try to drive as far as possible.

Roger put on a dazzling show. He connected on 10 of 14 passes for 161 yards and 2 touchdowns. One of his completions went for 51 yards, and another for 48 yards.

He impressed Landry with his poise, with the way he ran the team. He also did some running, scrambling for 28 yards. He once skittered about for so long a period of time that two Ram linemen fell from exhaustion.

"He reminds me of Fran Tarkenton," said Allen. "Except that Staubach, I believe, has a stronger arm."

Landry was even more encouraging. "There's no

doubt," the coach told the press, "that Roger will be a pro."

Before Roger left camp that summer, Landry spoke to him. "You have the makings of a professional quarterback," he said. "I didn't know what to expect when you arrived, but you have shown us something.

"You have a lot of things to learn; one of them is to control your running. But you have the essential qualities."

This was just what Roger was hoping to hear, a word of encouragement, an indication that he might have the necessary potential. He knew Landry to be an honest man. He knew that if he had not displayed the skills and temperament of a pro, Landry would have told him so. Roger wore a wide smile as he boarded the plane to Pensacola. He knew that he had proven something.

He had only been back a short time, when he read that the Cowboys had traded away Jerry Rhome, their No. 3 quarterback. Here was another vote of confidence. It was as if Landry were saying, "OK, Staubach, we think you can do it. Now show us." It made Roger more determined than ever to prove himself.

8 School Days as a Pro

Before Craig Morton had arrived upon the Dallas scene from the University of California, much less Roger, the Cowboys had suffered through many lean years, and the quarterback who led them—if that is the word—during those dismal days was Joe "Dandy" Don Meredith. When the Cowboys began to win over the regular season, but failed in title games, Dandy Don was still the man at the helm.

Dandy Don was big and strong-armed, and he played with courage and bravado. But to Meredith football was just a game, and while he could lash out at a lineman for missing a block or scream at a receiver for running the wrong pattern, he took most defeats with a shrug. Sure, the team had always flopped when the title seemed within its grasp, but, shucks, what could you do about that? "If ifs and buts were candy and nuts, we'd all have a Merry Christmas" was the way Meredith once put it.

This type of attitude did not endear Meredith to Coach Landry. When Meredith first came to the Cowboys, swaggering and spoiled, following a much-heralded career at SMU, the quarterback and the coach clashed frequently. Over the years the two had managed to develop an on-the-field working relationship, but the basic differences were still there.

In 1968, when Roger was doing his passing and running for the Goshawks, Dandy Don directed the Cowboys to a 12–2 season, which earned the team the championship of the Capitol Division of the Eastern Conference. Cleveland's Browns won the Century Division. The two faced one another in Cleveland one December day with the Conference title at stake.

Many of Meredith's passes ended up in the hands of Cleveland defensive backs that afternoon, and in the third quarter, when Meredith threw two of his interceptions, Landry removed him from the game and put in Morton. The Cowboys lost, 31–20.

One July day the next summer, Meredith, then thirty-one, not old for a quarterback, went to the Cowboy offices to talk with Landry. "I'm thinking of retiring," said Meredith, not quite sure how the coach would respond. Landry jumped to his feet. "Don," he said, reaching over to shake his hand, "I'm sure you're doing the right thing."

Craig Morton was driving along a California highway when his car radio informed him that Meredith was quitting. "How did you react?" a reporter asked him later. "It's a miracle," said Morton, "that there wasn't a whole string of wrecked automobiles along the highway."

Roger was in Pensacola awaiting his discharge when a phone call came from Curt Mosher, director of public relations for the Cowboys.

"Guess what?" said Mosher. "You've been traded!"

Roger gasped.

"No, I'm kidding," Mosher went on. "I'm calling to tell you that Meredith has quit."

There was silence on the other end.

When Roger, following his discharge, reported to the Cowboys' training camp in the summer of 1969, no one held out much hope for him. He was, after all, a rookie, and the failure rate among quarterback rookies was known to be very high, greater than fifty percent. What made it even tougher was the fact that Roger was no pink-cheeked young man right off the college campus. He was twenty-seven now, an age that set him apart from the other rookies. They kidded him about it, calling him "Dad" or saying, "Hey, Roger, I used to watch you when I was a kid." Roger took it good-naturedly, or at least he tried to.

In the early practice sessions, the coaches watched solemnly whenever Roger ran with the ball, and they would wag their heads from side to side and go, "Tsk . . . tsk . . . tsk," as if Roger were afflicted with some strange, incurable disease.

"Gonna get yourself killed someday doing that," they'd shout out. "Stay in the pocket!" But Roger felt that running was his way, his style. He couldn't change the way he played any more than he could alter the way he signed his name.

As if to prove that his way was the best way, Roger became the most tenacious of all the rookies—passing, running, dodging, scrapping. He was never still. The fury with which he played earned him a much bruised body, a few cracked bones, and a wrenched back. Ironically, the back injury happened while he was setting up to throw. For two or three weeks he was unable to follow through when he threw the ball, and his wild dashes became less wild.

Everyone was impressed by his dedication. Once he told a reporter that he was in such good shape that he thought he could run the 40-yard dash in 4.8 or 4.75, which was a second or so faster than his best college time.

The reporter asked a coach whether Roger, at twenty-seven, could be faster than he was at twenty-two or twenty-three. "If you want Staubach to run 4.75 for the forty-yard dash," the coach said, "all you've got to do is put him in a race with a guy who does 4.8."

Notre Dame's Bob Belden was another quarterback candidate in camp that summer. Roger and Belden would remain on the practice field for as long as they could get receivers to stay. Then late in the afternoon, with the sun casting long shadows across the field, Staubach would end the session by running a long fly pattern, racing straight down the center of the field, and Belden would wind up and fling the ball as far as he could. Roger, galloping under a full head of steam, would reach up and make the catch, yelling "Yee— oow!" and he'd never let up, keeping on a dead run all the way to the locker room more than a quarter of a mile away.

The departure of Dandy Don Meredith had not thrown the Cowboys into panic. Far from it. The dark and handsome Morton, blessed with a powerful arm (and cursed, some said, with a free spirit), came into camp determined to prove that he would run the show. Landry was much impressed. So were the players, and it wasn't long before they were believing that they could win with him.

Once during a practice session a player came into the huddle grumbling after a coach had pointed out a mistake the man had made. Morton didn't want to hear any grumbling. He grabbed the player by the shoulder pads. "I want to see you after practice!" Morton declared. No one could visualize Roger acting in a similar manner, not yet.

Morton's four years spent backing up Meredith had given him plenty of savvy. He had played often when Dandy Don was hurt. "I've been under the gun as much as any quarterback around," Morton was fond of saying. "I've been in situations where I've had to produce to win."

The quarterback job was Morton's; there was really no competition for it. As the Cowboys began playing out their schedule of exhibition games, Roger mostly watched.

He found it difficult to sit on the bench while someone else ran the team. It was a brand-new experience for him, and he took to it about the same way a wild colt takes to the bridle.

Landry had told Roger that it would be at least three years, and perhaps as many as five, before he had matured as a quarterback. But Roger didn't believe him. He had two years of experience at Pensacola behind him. He had been studying the Cowboy playbook for more than a year. He was in tiptop physical condition.

Roger wanted to play; indeed, he wanted to start, to be the No. 1 man. "Be patient, be patient," he had to keep telling himself.

Morton was competent as he steered the team to three wins in the first four preseason contests. On a hot and sultry night in Dallas, close to 75,000 showed up at the Cotton Bowl to watch the Cowboys play the New York Jets. Many in the huge throng had come to watch Joe Namath, but Broadway Joe's knees had been bothering him and he decided he wouldn't play. Late in the second quarter, while following through on a pass, Morton banged his hand on someone's helmet and he screamed in pain. He had dislocated a finger.

Roger went in. The Cowboys were trailing, 9–3,

and stalled on their own 24-yard line. There was one minute, 19 seconds left in the half.

Roger sent Walt Garrison barreling up the middle for 11 yards. He missed on a pass, then scrambled for 8 yards on second down. Calvin Hill took a handoff and slanted off right tackle for 5 yards and a first down on the Dallas 43. Now only 45 seconds remained in the half.

Roger completed a screen pass to Calvin Hill that netted 21 yards, and followed that with a completion to Lance Rentzel for an additional 16 yards. The crowd cheered him on. A bugle blared. "Charge!" roared the fans. Another pass went incomplete, stopping the clock. Twelve seconds remained.

Once more Roger drifted back to throw. He looked, couldn't find whatever it was he was looking for, paused, then scampered out of the pocket, feinted his way past John Elliot, and when he reached the goal line and found Ralph Baker blocking his path, Roger launched a flying leap, landing upside down in the end zone. Landry, one hand to a knitted brow, and staring at his feet, did not see it. The Cowboys went on to win convincingly, 23–9.

SUPER SUB HIJACKS PILOTLESS JETS screamed the headline in the Dallas *Morning News*. While he had moved the team well and showed that he could throw hard and with accuracy, frequently completing sideline passes where the margin for error is thin, Roger was less than super. Able, yes. Adequate, yes. But not super. There were times in the game that he was indecisive, and it was obvious that he was having problems reading defenses.

76

The next day the Cowboys learned that Morton would be out the following week when the Baltimore Colts would be in town, and he might not be available to face the St. Louis Cardinals in the season's opener. Landry predicted that Roger would have a harder time against the Colts than he had had against the Jets.

And Landry was right.

The best that could be said about Roger's performance against the Colts was that he pleased the fans, the Baltimore fans most of all. He broke from the pocket and ran with the ball no less than eleven times. The fans screamed in delight; Landry watched in horror.

Not only did Roger run too much, but his passing left a great deal to be desired. One newsman noticed that he was releasing the ball in sidearm fashion. Roger lost track of the number of times he was intercepted. When a reporter asked him after the game, why it was he got intercepted four times, Roger seemed stunned. "Four times!" he said. "Was I really intercepted four times? I never had that many in a game before. . . ." It was an easy win for Baltimore, 23–7. Roger went home that night a sad young man, realizing that he had a great deal to learn about professional football.

What had happened to Roger was the same thing that was happening to all the other young quarterbacks—the zone defense. Using a zone, the defense could stifle a team's passing attack—not obliterate it, but at least put a damper on its effectiveness. Baltimore was one of the best zone teams in pro football at the time.

What is a zone defense? The name is self-descriptive. It refers to a type of pass defense in which the players are assigned to cover a specific area of the field, a "zone," rather than a specific man.

As the quarterback drops back to pass, each of the defensive players races to his zone and each man stays there until the ball is thrown, whereupon they converge upon the intended receiver.

One early type of zone is shown here. The linebackers (L) retreat in one direction, and the safeties (S) and cornerbacks (C) in another. The effect is one of rotation, and, thus, this is called a rotating zone.

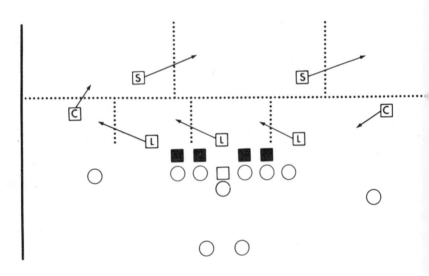

On one play, the defensive players may rotate in a clockwise direction (as shown here), but, on the next, their direction may be counterclockwise. The idea, of course, is to confuse the offense, the quarterback, in particular.

The zone defense had long been used in high school and college football, but the pros were slow to take to it. Instead, pro teams relied on the man-to-man defenses. Each of the cornerbacks was responsible for the wide receiver on his side; the strong-side safety covered the tight end. The outside linebackers helped out in the short pass area, while the middle linebacker stayed alert for screen passes or draw plays. As passers became more skilled and receivers faster and more artful, the man-to-man style of defense proved inadequate, especially on long passes. That's when teams began turning to the zone.

When a team was using a zone setup, a receiver might get a step or two advantage on a defenseman, but as he continued on his way, he entered another player's zone and thus would lose his edge. There was always a defensive man deep, and sometimes two of them, to cover on long passes. As a result, the word "bomb" was dropping out of football's lexicon.

Teams sophisticated in the use of the zone didn't employ it on every single play. In an effort to bewilder the passer, a team might use the zone on one play and a man-to-man alignment on the next.

Quarterbacks learned to cope with this. As the passer went back to throw, he would watch the strong safety. If the safety moved to cover the tight end, his normal assignment in a man-to-man defense, then the quarterback could be fairly certain that he was going to be throwing into a man-to-man setup. But if the strong safety slanted to either side or backpedaled, then defense was using the zone.

The zone defense was not perfect. In between the

areas of coverage, there were seams or gaps. The passer would seek to reach his receiver in one of these openings as the man crossed from one player's zone to another's. "The receiver is always open at some point" is the way George Blanda once put it. "It's up to the passer to throw the ball at the right spot at the right instant with just the right amount of snap on it."

This was approximately the state of the art during Roger's rookie year. Some teams were using the zone; most still clung to man-to-man. A small handful used both types and switched back and forth, but you could usually "read" which type of defense a team was going to employ, and then pass accordingly.

But things kept getting more complex.

The defense began disguising its moves. For example, the strong-side safety might fake a move in the direction of the tight end, making the quarterback think that man-to-man coverage was in use. But he would suddenly pull back into zone coverage.

Another thing that increased the quarterback's woes was that some teams began using zone and man-to-man coverage in combination. In one such combination, the linebackers handled the two running backs and the tight end on a man-to-man basis, while the defensive secondary covered in zone fashion.

There was more. Don Shula, before he left the Baltimore Colts as head coach to take the same job with the Miami Dolphins, developed a variation of the zone. Whereas the rotating zone established three areas of coverage deep and four shallow ones, Shula's new alignment called for five shallow zones and two deep. The cornerbacks came up to take the two outside short zones, the linebackers covered the three middle zones short, and the safeties took the two deep zones. Shula called his alignment the double zone. It made it extremely difficult for the passer to complete anything in the middle range, for, with all those defensemen between the passer and his receivers, it was like trying to throw through a picket fence.

What with the defensive players now masking their true actions, and the fact that there were now so many variations of the zone, the quarterback had a much more difficult chore of reading what type of defense he was facing. "The way they disguise these zones," said Joe Namath, "I wonder how a young quarterback can come into the league and survive; there's so much that goes into it, so much recognition. I wonder how I did it myself, except that they didn't try and hide the zone as much then."

What Namath and the other astute quarterbacks would do is attempt to read more than one defensive player. They would check the safeties first. If they divided and drifted back, it was a tipoff that the defense was using Shula's double zone. If the safeties went to the right or left, the rotating zone was being used.

The quarterbacks also checked what the linebackers were doing, too, especially the middle linebacker. If he was rotating to the left (while the deep backs were heading to the right), it was further evidence that a rotating zone was being used. A perceptive and experienced quarterback could sometimes get a clue as to what was coming even before the ball was snapped. As he walked up to the ball and called the signals, the quarterback might notice that the strong safety was lined up a bit deeper than normal, maybe only a step or two. This was because the man was going to cover deep on the play, and he had "cheated" a step or two so as to have a head start.

No wonder that Roger had his problems in his early months with the Cowboys. Not only was he expected to read the keys, but he also had to be able to react accordingly, throwing to the receiver who would be open. And he had to be able to do this not merely quickly but automatically, as if it were a reflex action, like swinging a bat at a pitched ball.

Lacking in experience and unable to always read what was happening, Roger relied on another method of attack. There was nothing subtle about it, nor was it based on his ability to perceive special information provided by scouts or the films or the game plan or anything like that. Roger simply put his head down and ran with the ball.

"I don't know exactly how to describe what happens out there," said Roger. "I just know that you have a feel for someone coming, and it's logical that you don't want to be there when he arrives."

Roger's tendency to run put him in conflict with Landry, who believed in the pocket theory. The quarterback was supposed to set up behind a protective cone of blockers and stay there. If the blocking broke down, then he was to allow himself to be flattened or throw the ball away, "dump" it. All of the more noted quarterbacks of the day—a group that included Sonny Jurgensen, Johnny Unitas, Earl Morrall, and Meredith—employed the pocket style.

Roger defended what he wanted to do. Running is a strength, he said. "If your receivers are blanketed and you can get an interception if you throw, what are you supposed to do?" he asked. "Eat the ball? Take a ten- or twelve-yard loss?

"I say, if you can run to the line of scrimmage, why not do it? Maybe when you get there you'll see some daylight."

Running also has value, said Roger, because it gives the defense something else to think about. "If they're waiting for the run, maybe your receivers can get open once or twice when they wouldn't otherwise."

Roger felt that his style was his own. He didn't want to be stereotyped. He didn't like it when people called him a scrambler. But he didn't want to be called a pocket passer either. He was a quarterback who ran with the ball.

The night before any home game, the Cowboys are quartered in the Hilton Hotel in Dallas. There, the coaches reason, the players can fully concentrate on the next day's task and not be distracted by wives, children, or, in the case of some, pretty girls or strong drink or both. The game plan is discussed; films may be shown.

So it was on the evening before the opening game in 1969. During the buffet dinner the team was served, Roger caught a glimpse of Landry staring at a wall, seemingly oblivious of all that was going on about him. Thinking the coach was unduly concerned about the prospect of having to start a rookie quarterback the following day, Roger sought to reassure him.

"Coach," he began, "do you realize that one year ago I was quarterbacking the Pensacola Goshawks, and we played teams such as Tennessee State and Murfreesboro, and tomorrow I'm going to be your quarterback against the St. Louis Cardinals."

Larry didn't say a word. He just turned and walked away.

Late in the first quarter, the game scoreless, the Cowboys got possession following a St. Louis punt, second down and five on their own 25-yard line. Landry sent in a pass play. The tight end was to break toward the inside, taking the safety with him. Wide receiver Lance Rentzel, running a down-and-out route, would thus be one-on-one with the cornerback on that side.

Rentzel was perfect. He threw a fake at the cornerback that froze him in his tracks, then he turned on the speed. Staubach threw. Running at full tilt, with the cornerback on his heels, Rentzel looked over his shoulder, and there was the ball. He put up his hands and brought it down, and kept right on running without breaking stride. He scored without anyone laying a hand on him. Roger Staubach in the first period of his first professional football game had completed a 75-yard touchdown pass.

During the second quarter, Roger seemed to be making a special effort to stay in the pocket. Twice he ate the ball, allowing himself to be dropped by enemy linemen. Not long before the period ended, Roger connected with Dennis Homan on another long pass, but Homan was pulled down from behind. The half ended with the Cowboys on top, 7–3.

Dallas got another touchdown in the third quarter when Calvin Hill took Roger's handoff, galloped to the right as if running a sweep, then suddenly stopped, stood erect, and uncorked a long pass to Rentzel who had gotten behind safety Larry Wilson. That gave Dallas a 14–3 lead.

If the Cards still believed they had a chance, Roger destroyed that hope in the final period. He drove the team into Cardinal territory to set up a field goal. After the Cards fumbled the ensuing kickoff, Roger, keeping to the ground to run out the clock, guided the team downfield once more. On second down from the St. Louis 4-yard line, Roger kept the ball and tried to sweep left end. He got only one yard before he was buried.

On third and three, Landry sent in a running play with Les Shy to do the carrying. But Shy ran the wrong way and missed the handoff, and suddenly Roger found himself holding the ball and without a blocker in sight. Instinctively, he broke to his left, against the flow. When Roger had about a yard to go, Rocky Rosema, a 230-pound linebacker, got his arms around Roger's legs. Roger lunged forward, then fell so that his head, shoulders, right arm, and the ball were across the goal line.

Landry praised Roger in the days that followed. He called him "a fine football player." He lauded Roger for "his fine arm and great determination." He hailed him for his outstanding ability as a runner. "Who's going to be your starting quarterback next week?" a reporter asked.

Landry looked at the man in surprise. "Morton, of course," Landry shot back.

"What's your feeling about Staubach?"

"There's no way that Roger could win the job this year. He has to learn our system, which is fairly complicated. He has to learn to read defenses.

"If," continued Landry, "later in the season, Staubach is No. 1, it will mean that it has been a lost season for us."

The next week Morton was the quarterback and Roger was on the bench, and that's the way it remained for the rest of the season. Roger got to throw the ball only 47 times.

But in those opening weeks of the 1969 season, Roger had accomplished a great deal. He had shown himself to be a solid performer. He could pass. He could also run. He could lead the team. What Roger had done was establish a beachhead.

Roger's second season with Dallas was pretty much a replay of the first. Morton was slow recovering from shoulder surgery, and Roger opened the season against the Eagles, guiding the team to a difficult win, 17–7. The following week against the Giants, Roger started again, and though the team made countless mistakes, they still managed to win, 28–10.

Against St. Louis the following week, Roger had difficulty—and that is putting it mildly—with Larry Wilson, the Cards' All Pro safety. Twice Wilson intercepted passes of Roger's. He was never where Roger expected him to be. Landry paced up and down and wore a pained expression.

About midway in the second period, with the score

3–0 in favor of the Cardinals, Landry decided he couldn't stand watching any longer. When Roger came off the field, Landry told him he was through for the day and that Morton was going in. Roger didn't know it at the time, but he was, in fact, through for the season.

The following Wednesday at his weekly press luncheon, Landry announced that he was going to start Morton against the Atlanta Falcons in Sunday's game and implied that he was going to stay with Craig for the rest of the season. "There are two reasons for going with Morton," Landry said. "One, Craig is throwing good again. He is not having the trouble he was having several weeks ago. Second, and most important, is his experience. Craig is able to read almost any defense and he can control our audible system and he keys effectively.

"This does not in any way downgrade Roger Staubach," Landry continued. "In my opinion, Roger is potentially a championship quarterback. The only thing he lacks at this point is experience; he's going into his second year.

"Even if we had to go with Roger this season, if Morton were injured or something, I think he'd do a doggone good job. He'd find a way to get the ball across the goal line."

Landry's mind was made up and there would be no changing it. It was simply that he knew what Morton could do. He wasn't yet sure about Roger.

More than once in weeks that followed, the Cowboys seemed to be headed for a sad season. By their ninth game they had lost four times.

Even though Morton's arm was giving him problems, real problems, Landry kept him in the lineup. He simply believed that Morton's experience was more valuable than whatever contribution Roger might be able to make.

It pained Roger to read newspaper stories saying that the quarterback position was the Cowboys' weak spot. He felt he could make it a strong position. All he wanted was the opportunity to get in there and show them.

Suddenly, when everyone was saying that the Cowboys were finished, they began winning. They ended the season with five straight victories, which enabled them to capture a playoff berth.

The Cowboys then downed the Lions, 5–0, to win the right to play the 49ers for the Conference title. By controlling the ball with a rock-ribbed ground game and by blitzing enough to keep John Brodie off balance, the Cowboys came out on top, 17–10.

The Super Bowl, with the Colts the opposition, was wild and weird. Morton threw two painful interceptions, which, combined with a fumble, killed the Cowboys' chances. A 32-yard field goal by Baltimore's Jim O'Brien with five seconds to play was the deciding factor.

Dallas had run true to form; they had blown it.

Roger watched what happened from the sidelines, hardly moving, not saying a word. In the game's statistics, he, along with Tony Liscio, a reserve tackle, were listed under the category DNP—DID NOT PLAY.

Roger knew that he could never let it be like that again. No way.

9 Quarterback Carousel

Roger got to Dallas from the Super Bowl on Monday. The next day he was out on the practice field alone, throwing footballs at a practice board. Later in the week he showed up at the club offices requesting that films be taken of his workouts so that he could study his moves.

The coaching staff hadn't yet recovered from the Super Bowl debacle. "My God!" said Ermal Allen, one of Landry's assistants. "You've got six months to get ready!"

"I don't have six months," said Staubach. "And I'm ready now. If I don't start or play this season, it will be my last with the Cowboys."

Roger was twenty-nine now; in February he was going to be thirty. Many players, at thirty, are beginning to concentrate their efforts at getting set up in business, and often their greatest concern is how many years they've accrued toward the players' pension fund.

Fran Tarkenton, only two years older than Staubach, was about to begin his eleventh season as a first-string quarterback. Joe Namath, a year younger, was debating whether to retire.

Landry decided very early in the year that Roger would be given an opportunity to win the No. 1 assignment. As the new season approached, he said: "This year we have to reestablish a leader at quarterback, like Meredith was. Craig hung in there tough in a trying situation last season. But he'll have to deliver.

"This is the year that Roger could make his move to take over as starting quarterback. Let them prove it on the field. I'm planning to alternate them as starters in the preseason, beginning with Morton against the Rams."

The preseason games settled nothing. Sometimes Landry would split up a game so that Morton worked the first and third quarters, and Roger the second and fourth. Other times he'd divide a game down the middle, one half for Morton, one half for Roger. So it went, with the Cowboys playing six games—against Los Angeles, New Orleans, Cleveland, Houston, Baltimore, and Kansas City—and winning all six. What they proved was that they were a very good football team.

After each game, Landry and his assistants would carefully evaluate the performance of each quarterback, and now, with six games in the books, Landry announced that his decision concerning the Morton-Staubach situation was to make no decision. The coach said he was going with "two No. 1 quarterbacks," and that in the rotating system that he planned Roger would be given the first start. No one quite understood how Landry had arrived at this settlement, and his explanation to the press didn't really clarify it.

"I'm very satisfied with Craig's progress," Landry

said. "He's made great strides in coming back. He's throwing the ball as well as he ever threw it. He has a lot of confidence in himself and his production has been very good—good enough for us to win. I could not be more satisfied with Morton at this point of the season.

"As for Roger, he came into the summer knowing that he had to make great strides to offset his inexperience. I think he has made great strides. You watch him work, and he demonstrates poise, and he doesn't scramble much; he reads defenses and hits people, all of which he couldn't do last year.

"I have said that a backup man could not replace a starter without superiority over him, a clear-cut superiority. Roger does not possess that superiority at this time. Therefore, Morton does not lose his starting status with us and this is the reason I have gone to the two quarterback situation."

If the practice of using two quarterbacks in pro football has ever been successful, evidence of it has been lost to history. Landry's own coaching philosophy had always been to turn the job over to one man and let him sink or swim with it. Every other coach operated the same way. Of course, a team must carry two quarterbacks; that is as basic to the game as cleats and two goalposts. But the ranking of each must be clearly established. One man must be the starter, the other his understudy. When each is given equal eminence, the coach is asking for trouble.

Anytime it has been tried, it has lead to divisiveness. When the Los Angeles Rams split the quarterbacking job between Norm Van Brocklin and Bob Waterfield in the early 1950's, there was frequently open hostility between the two. George Wilson, coach of the Detroit Lions in the early 1960's, shuttled quarterbacks Milt Plum and Earl Morrall in and out of the lineup, and he once chose the starting quarterback for a game on the basis of a coin flip. Wilson's indecisiveness wrecked the team.

The problem with the two quarterback system is that the man who's in the game realizes that the quarterback on the sidelines is, so to speak, looking over his shoulder, waiting for him to make a mistake. This inhibits him; he's afraid to take a chance. Suppose the quarterback faces a third-and-three situation. The book says to call a running play, something off tackle or maybe an inside trap. But once in a while when it's third-and-three, the quarterback might want to throw the ball in an effort to cross up the defense. Well, a quarterback who's involved in a competitive situation isn't going to throw. He knows that if the pass goes awry, the other man is going to be sent in as his replacement.

So neither man feels he has any freedom. This is the way it was in Detroit with Milt Plum and Earl Morrall. More recently, it was the situation that prevailed in Washington where Redskin Coach George Allen had two quarterbacks of about equal skill in Sonny Jurgensen and Bill Kilmer. As the 1972 season got under way, Allen named Jurgensen the starter. In an early season game against the Giants, Sonny suffered a torn Achilles' tendon, which sidelined him for the rest of the year. When Kilmer took over, he was a cooler, more confident quarterback than he had ever been before in his life, and he admitted that a principal reason for the improvement was that he knew that he could free-wheel, that even if he made a mistake there was no chance that he would be yanked.

Another difficulty with the two quarterback system is that when you divide the job of quarterbacking, you also divide the team. Some players favor one man, some favor the other. And the fans get split up into opposing camps, too. It's a bad situation all around.

When Roger heard that Landry was planning to use two quarterbacks, the news didn't cause him great joy, yet he couldn't help but feel that it was a vote of confidence, evidence that he was making some progress. "I'm better off than I was," he said.

Don Meredith happened to be in Dallas at the time Landry made his feelings known, and he was loud in his criticism of his former coach. He called it a "wishy-washy decision." If he were the coach, Meredith said, "I would go with Morton the whole way, or until he stunk up the place so bad that he couldn't cut it.

"It's Landry's responsibility as head coach to pick a quarterback. After he picks him, it's his responsibility to go with him. Now after he's spent this long with them and he doesn't have an idea which one is best, then get another coach."

The matter of who would quarterback the Cowboys was not the only problem that Landry was seeking to solve. Duane Thomas, the sensational rookie running back, who had originally signed a three-year contract, felt that he was worthy of a raise and he asked the Cowboys to tear up his contract and write a new one. When the club refused, Thomas called Landry a "plastic man," and he said that General Manager Tex

Schramm was "sick, demented, and completely dishonest." Schramm laughed off the criticism, saying, "That's not bad; he got two out of three."

Before the week was out, Thomas was traded to the New England Patriots. At the Patriots' training camp in Amherst, Massachusetts, Coach John Mazur told Thomas to get down in a three-point stance. Thomas said he preferred the two-point style and he demonstrated it to Mazur. "This is how we did it in Dallas," he declared, "and this is how I'm going to do it here." Mazur ordered him off the field. Indeed, he ordered him out of Amherst and all the way back to Dallas. But Duane refused to rejoin the club unless the Cowboys prepared a new contract. However, before the opening game of the season, Thomas softened his stand and rejoined the team.

Landry was also feuding with Bob Hayes over contract terms. The previous season Hayes had played out his option, and now he was insisting that he wanted to be traded. Wide receiver Lance Rentzel, suffering personal problems, had been dealt to the Los Angeles Rams for Lance Alworth, a pass receiver of superior skills.

On the plus side, the running fame was bolstered by the fact that the frequently injured Calvin Hill was healthy. And even if Duane Thomas did quit, the reliable Walt Garrison was ready to take his place.

The defense, bulwarked by a front four of Jethro Pugh, Bob Lilly, George Andrie, and Larry Cole, still ranked as the league's best. The linebackers, Chuck Howley, Lee Roy Jordan, and Dave Edwards, were said to be aging, but no one doubted they were still capable of doing an outstanding job. Age stalked the secondary, too, with cornerback Herb Adderley and safety Cornell Green heading into their eleventh seasons. The offensive line was coming back intact.

Many forecasters picked the Cowboys to win their division title, and a good number predicted they could capture the Super Bowl—but only if Landry managed to unravel the quarterback situation.

As it worked out, Roger wasn't able to start the opening game of the season—against the Buffalo Bills —because of a ruptured blood vessel in his thigh. Landry was afraid he would aggravate the injury. Morton would start, then Roger would be used the following week against the Philadelphia Eagles.

The Buffalo game was a wild affair, with the young, enthusiastic Bills throwing a scare into the Cowboys, who were favored by 2 touchdowns. The Bills actually led, 30–28, in the third quarter, but the Cowboy offense began turning assorted Buffalo misplays into touchdowns, and pulled away. The final score: Dallas, 49; Buffalo, 37. "Glad to get out of there," said Landry.

Roger prepared diligently for the game against the Eagles, studying the thick scouting report, with its pages of statistics, charts, and diagrams, memorizing it, so that by the time the Cowboys arrived in Philadelphia, he felt he knew the Eagles at least as well as their own coaching staff, perhaps better. Put it down as wasted effort. On the second play from scrimmage, Staubach fired over the middle; his target was tight end Mike Ditka. But Ditka was held up by a block and Bill Bradley intercepted.

has happened to me since I've been playing football. Roger had released the ball, he was standing there with tackle Ralph Neely, when suddenly Mel Tom, the Eagles' big—6 feet 4, 250 pounds—defensive end, grabbed Roger by the arm, spun him around, and then, using his forearm, began clubbing him in the jaw. Roger fell to the ground and he didn't get up. Morton was rushed in.

They helped Roger to the sidelines, and there he stood for the rest of the afternoon as Morton fashioned a 42–7 victory, completing 15 of 22 passes for 188 yards. When the game's outcome was assured, Landry took Morton out and put Dan Reeves in. Reeves had been a wide receiver, a running back and an assistant coach. The game in Philadelphia marked his debut as a quarterback.

It was a long plane ride home for Roger. His jaw throbbed and his head ached. Worse, he couldn't help but think after working so hard all summer, indeed, all year, his opportunity was slipping from his grasp, and all because of a defensive end named Mel Tom. The next week Morton was scheduled to start against the Redskins. What would happen if the Cowboys won again, Roger thought, and won convincingly? Would Landry then feel committed to using Morton the following week? How could he really do otherwise? It could go like that for the entire season.

When Roger and the other Cowboys saw the film depicting Mel Tom's attack, it seemed to them that the Eagle player had been guilty of the cheapest of cheap shots. "I can't believe it," said Roger. "They should have thrown him out of the game. Nothing like this has happened to me since I've been playing football.

"They ought to fine him . . . and give the money to me."

Later in the week, Landry confirmed that Morton would open as quarterback in the game against the Redskins. "Roger just hasn't competed the last two weeks," Landry said. "It's not his fault; he's just had some tough luck."

Roger didn't need to be reminded.

Even though Washington had not yet been beaten, the odds-makers had established the Cowboys an eight-point favorite. People had not yet begun to take the team seriously. George Allen, the Redskin coach, had assembled what was being called his Over the Hill Gang, and he did it by trading away his draft choices for veteran players. "I like to see bald heads on my squad," he said. Football traditionalists laughed at Allen. The tried and proven method of building a winning team was through the draft, they claimed, going about the task slowly, year by year, and maybe it took three or four years, but it was the surer method. But Allen was to demonstrate that you could do it his way, too, and he was to demonstrate it very clearly in the game against the Cowboys.

Running back Charlie Harraway scored on the third play of the game to jump the Redskins into the lead. Washington scored a second touchdown in the second quarter on a Bill Kilmer pass to Roy Jefferson, the play covering 50 yards. Meanwhile, Morton could do little, and in the fourth quarter, with the Redskins ahead, 20–9, Landry pulled Morton and sent Roger in.

The Cowboys were 69 yards away from the Redskin

end zone, but Roger's pinpoint passes brought the team downfield quickly. Three times he targeted on tight end Mike Ditka and he connected each time. With the ball only a yard from the goal line, Roger handed off to Calvin Hill, who bulled his way through for a touchdown. Mike Clark booted the extra point and the gap was down to four points.

Three minutes were left. As the Cowboys kicked off, Roger and the other members of the offensive team huddled in front of the Cowboy bench and Roger called the first two plays of the next series. One problem remained for the Cowboys—to get the ball back. They never solved it. Running backs Larry Brown, Charlie Harraway, and Tommy Mason kept grinding out first downs, and all Roger and his teammates could do was stand there and watch the clock run out.

The New York Giants were next, a night game in the Cotton Bowl. Roger started. It was a bizarre game, filled with fumbles, costly penalties, and other similar horrors. "Complete ineptitude" Howard Cosell told his nationwide football audience.

Time and time again Roger brought the Cowboys downfield, but misplays prevented him from getting the ball across the goal, at least they did until late in the second quarter when he connected with tight end Billy Truax for a touchdown. The score was 13–6 in the Cowboys' favor when Roger came off the field at halftime. Landry thought the team should have been ahead by a much greater margin, and in the locker room he announced, "Morton will play the second half." He made one other important change, putting Duane Thomas in the lineup to replace Walt Garrison.

Thomas, with his bruising power and speed, tipped the scales in the Cowboys' favor during the second half, averaging 6.6 yards per carry on 9 carries. Dallas won, 20–13.

During the ensuing week Landry announced that Morton would start against New Orleans on Sunday, and Roger would be the starter the following week against the New England Patriots. Morton had a trying time against the Saints, getting intercepted twice, once in the New Orleans' end zone. The second time it happened the Saints ran the ball back 60 yards.

New Orleans was not rated as one of the league's powerhouse teams, and everyone had said the game was going to be a piece of cake, but at the end of the second period, the scoreboard read: New Orleans, 17; Dallas, 0. The third quarter had hardly begun when Landry sent Roger in.

It was an uphill struggle, but Roger almost made it. He completed 7 of his first 10 passes, one a 41-yarder to Gloster Richardson for a touchdown, and another to Bob Hayes, good for 18 yards and a second touchdown.

The Cowboys now trailed by only 3 points. There were ten minutes left, plenty of time. The Saints were forced to punt. Charlie Waters, back to receive, signaled fair catch—then fumbled. The Saints recovered. Minutes later New Orleans had to punt again. This time Cliff Harris, standing deep in Dallas territory, did the fumbling, and the Saints turned the misplay into a touchdown and a 24–14 win.

The situation was getting grim. The Cowboys had 3 wins and 2 losses to show for the season, while the Redskins were yet to lose, and thereby held a 2-game lead in the Eastern Division. The whole Cowboy team was grousing about the quarterback situation. Some players hoped that Landry would settle on Roger, while others favored Morton. But Ralph Neely summed up the team's overall feeling best when he declared, "It would help to have one quarterback. Either damn one. At this point I don't care."

The Cowboys had always played their home games in the Cotton Bowl, but the game against New England was to be their first in their new home, Texas Stadium in Irving, Texas, a kind of Taj Mahal of pro football. It is unusual for two reasons—for its great open dome and for the fact that it was built from money put up by Cowboy fans. They were asked to purchase $250 bonds (which were to return $300 in thirty-five years), and by so doing they received an option to purchase season tickets.

The more bonds a fan purchased, the better his choice of seats, although the word "seats" is misleading. Purchasing $50,000 in bonds gave one the opportunity to buy one of the 170 "inner circle suites," each about the size of a motel room, with one glass wall overlooking the playing field. The owner of a suite was permitted to purchase twelve season tickets. Promoted by the Cowboys as "your 'personal penthouse' at Texas Stadium, similar to a second residence, like a lake home or a ranch," the suites sold quickly. Many of them were luxuriously furnished by their owners. There were suites with beamed ceilings and parquet floors, with crystal chandeliers and oak-paneled bars, and one suite owner boasted Louis XIV couches and gilt chairs.

Of course, individual seats cost far less than the suites. Those beyond the 30-yard lines went for a $250 bond, plus $63 for a season ticket. Approximately 15,000 seats deep in the end zones were to be made available on a game-by-game basis at $7 apiece.

The Cowboys' locker room featured fine wood paneling and thick carpeting, giving it a country-club appearance. Seats in the press box were upholstered in soft leather. A television screen was mounted between each pair of seats so that journalists could watch instant replays. The most stunning feature of the stadium was its great vaulted roof which covered everything but the playing field.

More than 65,000 fans filled the stadium to watch Roger lead the Cowboys against the Patriots, a hapless team at the time. It was a game in which the offense could no nothing wrong. On the fourth play from scrimmage, Duane Thomas burst 56 yards for a touchdown. Roger was never better, scoring one touchdown himself on a 2-yard run and passing to Bob Hayes for 2 others. So explosive was the Cowboy attack, that they led 34–7 at the half; it ended, 44–21.

Lyndon Johnson had been a spectator, and after the game he visited the Cowboy locker room to congratulate the players. When he shook Roger's hand, he said, "You sure know how to break in a new stadium." Everyone agreed. Roger had put on a virtuoso performance.

The Bears were to be the opposition the next week,

101

with the game to be played in Chicago. Roger knew that it was supposed to be Morton's "turn" to start, but he thought that perhaps, on the basis of his splendid showing against the Patriots, Landry might give him first call. He was thus wholly unprepared for what the coach was planning.

Early in the week Landry announced that Morton would not be the quarterback for the game. But neither would Staubach. Instead, they were going to divide the game play-by-play, using a shuttle system.

Morton, said Landry, would quarterback the first play of every series and Staubach the second, and they would continue to alternate on ensuing downs. Quarterback schizophrenia had reached its loftiest heights.

When Landry announced that he was going to use a quarterback shuttle system, he also said that he would be calling the plays. He had begun doing so the previous week in the game against the Patriots ("I'm going to help Roger a little," he explained), using tight ends Billy Truax and Mike Ditka and his messengers, sending one in for the other on each down. Now he would simply let either Morton or Staubach carry in the play he would use.

The Cowboys could hardly believe their ears when they learned that Landry was planning to shift quarterbacks on each play. None would allow himself to be quoted on the topic.

The Bears, however, were more than happy to comment. "Landry's got to be kidding," said Ed O'Bradovich, a defensive end. "That has got to help us." Linebacker Doug Buffone said, "Landry must be cracking up."

As Landry expressed it, the strategy was meant to confuse the Chicago defense, but it was Morton and Staubach who appeared bewildered the most. The Bears intercepted 4 of their passes, turning 2 of them into field goals. There were 4 fumbles, and 3 of these ended up in the hands of Chicago players. What was surprising about the game was that the Cowboys managed to stay close, the Bears winning by only 4 points, 23–19.

The defeat gave Dallas a 4-3 record. The Redskins, leading the division, were 6-1. The season had reached a dismal low point. Landry knew he had to end the game of musical chairs.

On the Tuesday night after the Cowboys lost to the Bears, Roger was at home when the phone rang. It was Landry. "I'm making you the No. 1 quarterback," Landry said. "It's up to you now."

10 Player of the Year

"Fantastic! It's fantastic!"

That's how Roger greeted the news that Landry was making him the team's No. 1 quarterback, not merely for the upcoming game against the Cards, but for the balance of the season.

"This is the first time I'm *really* the quarterback," said Roger. "I'm not walking the tightrope anymore. If I make a few mistakes, I'll still be in there."

When it came to throwing the ball, handing off, and

all the other skills that the position of quarterback requires—what coaches call "the tools"—Staubach and Morton were about equal; if anything, Morton had the edge. But there was one essential difference, an almost indefinable thing, yet very real. Staubach could make the Cowboys move. So could Morton, but not nearly as well.

"I thought that the team would rally around Staubach," Landry was to reveal several months later. "It was a psychological thing more than anything else."

The term "psychological thing" could be reduced to one word—leadership. Ordinarily, it takes a young quarterback several years before a pro team is ready to accept him as a leader. He has to be able to demonstrate his intelligence to the team and the fact that he has a thorough understanding of the offensive system being used. He has to show that he has plenty of confidence. Roger's ability to lead was developed during his years at the Naval Academy and, before that, at NMMI.

The Cowboys believed in Roger. They looked upon him as the team's motive force, what made it go.

"I was living in Baltimore when Staubach was in the Navy," says teammate Calvin Hill. "What a leader! I can feel the leadership in him by osmosis.

"If I were a running back, I'd be afraid even if he were third or fourth string and I knew he was after my job. He's got that kind of spirit."

The ability to lead becomes apparent—or fails to—when a quarterback has moved his team inside the opposition's 20-yard line. The defense digs in, resolving to make the quarterback settle for a field goal. How often the quarterback succeeds in getting his team beyond the goal line is a valid test of his skill as a leader. It's a pity that the NFL doesn't keep statistics on the subject.

You can also judge a quarterback's ability to lead by what he is able to get out of a team when it is pinned down behind its own 20-yard line. The defense is fired up; their aim is to keep the team bottled up deep within its own territory, forcing a mistake, hopefully a turnover.

Some quarterbacks have a natural ability to lead; they're born with it. Others acquire the skill. When it comes to naming the game's "naturals," the name of Johnny Unitas has to be at the top of the list or very close to it. From the day he joined the Colts in 1956, he was the team's undisputed leader. The way he barked out signals, the cold-eyed look he'd give a receiver who ran the wrong pattern, the confidence he had, the faith in himself and his skills, were an inspiration to Baltimore teams for more than a decade and a half. And even in his last years with the team, when his arm often ached and his passes had a crazy wobble, he was still assured, almost arrogant, and this is what enabled him to get the job done.

Joe Namath was a great deal like Unitas. When Namath stepped out on the field, you *knew* he was the leader. The team seemed more alert, more willing to respond.

Bart Starr, who achieved enormous success with the Green Bay Packers, is an example of the quarterback who learns to be a leader. In his early years with Green Bay, Starr was quiet and reserved. He called a careful game, seldom taking any chances. He knew his job; he had the tools. He also had a team that hardly ever won. Few people realize that the Packers lost 9 games of 12 in Starr's first full year as the team's quarterback. Then Vince Lombardi took over at Green Bay and endowed Starr with what he was later to call "mental toughness." Lombardi, a demanding, driving person, would not accept second best. Starr became an on-the-field extension of Lombardi.

Bob Griese of the Miami Dolphins was cut from much the same pattern as Bart Starr. He's a fine leader, but he's acquired his qualities of leadership.

"Roger Staubach has true leadership," according to Tex Schramm, president and general manager of the Cowboys. "The other players see it and respect it. It's just there—self-assurance, confidence, maturity—whatever it is that defines leadership."

The St. Louis game was a nail-biter. The Cowboys moved the ball well in the first two quarters but were unable to score.

Yet Roger was unworried. He knew that it was his game to win or lose. That's what Landry had told him (although he had stressed *win*). Roger wasn't looking over his shoulder to see whether Morton was warming up. As long as it was up to him, Roger believed, everything would turn out fine.

The Cowboys trailed by a 10–3 score at the end of the second quarter and were still behind, 10–6, as the final quarter opened. Then Roger put together the Cowboys' only touchdown drive, using Duane Thomas to skirt the ends, passing to Lance Alworth, and running the ball himself. For the touchdown, he threw to Mike Ditka, the play covering four yards.

St. Louis came back with a field goal to tie the score at 13–13. With only mintues left, Roger marched the Cowboys downfield once more, hitting Alworth on his sixth, seventh, and eighth passes of the game. The clock showed 1:43 to play when Toni Fritsch, who had recently been activated by the Cowboys, booted the game-winning field goal.

The plane trip home was further brightened by the news that the Redskins had been tied by the Eagles. The next week, as the Cowboys breezed by the Eagles, the Redskins lost to the Bears. Thus, with five weeks remaining on the season, the standings on the Eastern Division of the National Conference looked like this:

	Won	*Lost*	*Tied*	*Percentage*
Washington Redskins .	6	2	1	.750
Dallas Cowboys	6	3	0	.667
New York Giants	4	5	0	.444
St. Louis Cardinals . . .	3	6	0	.333
Philadelphia Eagles. . .	2	6	1	.250

Obviously, it had boiled down to a two-team race. The following week the two teams were to meet at Washington's home grounds, Robert F. Kennedy Stadium.

Newspaper reporters and television broadcasters like to establish "turning points" for games. If the Washington game had one, it came in the first period, Dallas in possession, the ball on the Redskin 29-yard line. The play was to be a pass, with Alworth and Hayes lining up on the left side. Alworth was to run a down and in pattern, while Hayes was to go deeper, shooting straight downfield and then veering toward the goalpost. When Roger cocked his arm to throw, he noticed two things—that his receivers were tightly covered and that the area between him and the goal line was almost vacant. So Roger ran—all the way to Washington end zone for the game's only touchdown. Mike Clark, replacing the injured Toni Fritsch, booted a pair of field goals and the Cowboys won, 13–0.

Staubach ran the ball four times in the game, gaining 49 yards. Landry was having a difficult time getting used to it. "I guess Roger still can't see the open receivers" was one of his comments.

But no one else was doing any complaining. Since being named the starting quarterback, Roger had directed the team in three games and they had won all three. More important, the team was now functioning as a unit, with each man confident in the other.

Steve Perkins, who covered the team for a Dallas newspaper and chronicled the Cowboys' season in a book titled *Winning the Big One,* wrote at this juncture: "At certain parts of every season there is a *sense* of the team that is almost tangible, made up of bits and pieces, a gesture here, a word there, and now I had the feeling Dallas would not lose a game the rest of the way to the playoffs."

Roger would have agreed with this estimate. "The Redskin game was the game," he was to say later, "in which I really took command of the club."

If there was any cloud in the sky at this point, it was

Landry's continuing practice of calling the plays. He alternated tight ends Billy Truax and Mike Ditka, using them to carry in his "message."

While much has been written of Landry's wish to call the plays for his quarterback, little has been said that is complimentary. The system is supposed to rob a quarterback of his initiative, make him a robot.

There are, however, several arguments in favor of the policy. The obvious one is that the coach knows the formations and plays better than anyone else, and he is better qualified to choose the appropriate one of each for the situation at hand. This is particularly true in the case of the Cowboys, who feature a multiple offense. It is also well known that the coach makes his judgment not merely on whatever happens to strike his fancy, but that it is based on a pool of information, information collected from the quarterbacks (the one in the game and the one on the sidelines), and the coaches in the press box.

There is one other point, often overlooked. Landry, before the ball is snapped, informs (by telephone) the coaches in the press box as to what the play is going to be. They know what is going to happen (or is supposed to happen) before it happens. They are thus able to focus their attention on the point of attack, and if the play works or it doesn't, they know why. Maybe someone missed a block or perhaps the defense adjusted to stop the play. Obviously, information of this type has great value.

I have stood on the sidelines at Landry's elbow and watched the system work, and occasionally I've been able to overhear the call. When you know the play beforehand, you become suddenly endowed with enormous insight. You know just where to look; you know exactly what to look for. So it is with the coaching staff. They're able to detect things that usually aren't revealed to them until they have had an opportunity to screen the game films.

Under the Landry system, the quarterback does not necessarily have to follow the coach's direction. He has the option of changing the play.

When the team breaks from the huddle, Roger scans the defense. If he sees that the defensive players are so aligned that they are going to be able to stop the play, he can switch to another of his own choosing. He does this with an audible—the term used to designate the verbal signal he gives to alert the team that he is going to call a new play. He audibles as he bends over the center, waiting for the snap, then follows with the verbal signal for the new play. Roger usually audibles four or five times in a game.

When Roger took over as the Cowboy quarterback, his first inclination was to rebel at the coach's insistence on doing the play-calling. He felt that the policy implied that he, Roger, wasn't capable of knowing which play to call. The system thus cast doubts on his intelligence, his leadership qualities.

Then Roger began to analyze the situation, trying to be as objective as possible. First off, he was now the No. 1 quarterback for one of the best teams in professional football. Second, he *was* inexperienced as a pro, having played in only a handful of games.

Third, Landry had to be considered one of the best coaches in the business, possessed with a "genius mind," as Roger has put it. Fourth, the team was winning.

So, after Roger considered the facts, he decided his distress was being caused by his ego. What he had to do, he told himself, was to learn to accept his role. He had to learn to obey—just as he had at the Academy, just as he had during his boyhood years.

In another season, he would make an issue of it. Right now, he would go along. The team was winning. Why rock the boat? But next year. . . .

On Thanksgiving Day the Cowboys faced the Los Angeles Rams in Texas Stadium. The Rams had the most plays, the most yards, most time with the football, and most everything else of importance. What they didn't have was the most points at the end. The Cowboys came out on top, 28–21, their fourth straight win and a victory that put them a full game ahead of the Redskins.

Roger's ability to make the big play was never more apparent. The Cowboys were flat in the early stages, yet they managed to leave the field at halftime with a 14–14 tie, one of the touchdowns coming on a 51-yard pass from Staubach to Bob Hayes.

After a pass from Roger to Lance Alworth earned the Cowboys a third touchdown, quarterback Roman Gabriel put together a long drive for the Rams, which made the score 21–21. After the kickoff, Roger brought the Cowboys down the field again. A key play was his 11-yard run for the 17-yard line. Duane Thomas scored the touchdown and that was the ball game. Roger was now batting 1.000—5 hits in 5 attempts.

Landry had called the game against the Rams not merely a key game but "a super key game." "If we win this one," he explained, "we're in the driver's seat"— the implication being that the Cowboys were not expected to have great difficulty with the remaining teams they were to face—the Jets, the Giants, and the Cards.

The Jets, however, were not to be taken lightly. Joe Namath was back in the lineup, having returned to action after suffering a leg injury in preseason play. His first appearance of the season had come the previous week against a heavily favored San Francisco team, and he had thrown a terrible scare into the 49ers with his long and accurate passes. The Jets had come very close to winning.

In the game against the Cowboys, Namath might just as well have stayed in his New York town house. The Jets were bludgeoned at the start and never recovered. Ike Thomas, a rookie from Bishop College in Dallas, ran back the opening kickoff 101 yards. Namath was unable to get the Jets moving. After they punted, Roger steered the Cowboys downfield quickly. With the ball on the New York 27-yard line, Roger faked a pitchout to his left, then turned and spotted Calvin Hill all alone on the right side. The throw was perfect and the catch was easy. Hill raced into the end zone.

The Jets saw more of Roger's guile the next time the Cowboys got possession. Again the ball was on the New York 27-yard line. Roger faked a handoff to

Duane Thomas, then suddenly stood erect and rifled another scoring pass to Calvin Hill.

The Cowboys had 28 points before the game was one-quarter gone. Namath was taken out before the end of the period. "It was the coach's decision," Namath said. "However, he didn't get an argument from me."

After the game, New York Assistant Coach Buddy Ryan labeled Roger a "different type" of scrambler. "Fran Tarkenton lays down before you can hit him," said Ryan. "This guy Staubach thinks he's a running back. He plays like he's a running back. He plays like he's still trying to win the Heisman Trophy in the pros."

The previous week Roger had ranked as the No. 1 passer in the National Conference, according to statistics compiled by League headquarters. In the game against the Jets, he added to his statistical eminence by completing 10 passes in 15 attempts for 168 yards and 3 touchdowns.

The following week the Cowboys manhandled the other New York team, the Giants. With their 42–14 win, the Cowboys assured themselves of a playoff berth. The victory gave them a 10–3 record and a one-and-one-half game lead over the Redskins, with just one more game to play.

Roger riddled the New York defenses with his passes, completing 10 of 14 for 232 yards and 3 touchdowns. One pass stood out. The Cowboys were in possession on their own 15-yard line, second down, 2 yards to go for a first down. Anticipating a pass, the Giants blitzed in, chasing Roger into the end zone where linebacker Ron Hornsby got his hands on him. But Roger pulled free, retreated to the back line of the end zone, and then wound up and threw the ball about as hard as he could. Bob Hayes, racing straight down the middle of the field with a Giant defender on each shoulder, looked up and there was the ball. As the three players crossed the New York 35-yard line, Hayes reached up. There was a brief struggle and suddenly Hayes burst free, and he raced the rest of the way without being challenged. A chorus of "oohs" and "aahs" came from the stunned crowd. No wonder— Roger's throw had covered more than 70 yards.

Locker space on the Cowboys, as on most teams, is delegated on the basis of uniform number, and thus, Roger, No. 12, and Morton, No. 14, had adjacent lockers (there being no No. 13 on the Cowboy squad). This fact was beginning to make for some difficult moments. As the Cowboys began to win consistently, reporters would cluster about Roger after a victory and virtually ignore Craig. It kept getting worse. Toward the end of the season, great hordes of newsmen would inundate Roger and crowd Morton out of his cubicle.

Roger realized what was happening and how difficult it must have been on Craig. "I understand how he must feel," he said.

Yet Roger was realistic. "But that's what it's all about isn't it?—who's playing well. What's happening to Craig could be happening to me."

Duane Thomas was about the whole story in the final game of the regular season. With the Cardinals the opposition, Thomas ripped off a 53-yard touchdown run early in the first quarter, and 2 more scoring gallops in the second quarter. After that, it was easy.

Now the Cowboys were champions of the Eastern Division of the National Football Conference. Of course, the title wouldn't have much meaning unless the team could manage to win the next three games—a playoff game against the Vikings the next week, the Conference championship the week after that, and then the one game that was the focal point of the entire season, the Super Bowl.

On Christmas Day the Cowboys met the Vikings. Amazingly, the temperature in Bloomington was a balmy thirty degrees. Just as amazingly, the field was in A-1 condition.

The Cowboys' strategy for the game was no dark secret. The Vikings' Purple People Eaters, their front four—Carl Eller and Jim Marshall, the ends; Gary Larsen and Alan Page, the tackles—were the best defensive line in the league, adept at stopping runs cold and throttling down any passing attack. So what the Cowboys had to do was make no mistakes. "You can't feel that you're going to hit big plays or have a consistent attack against a defense like this one," Landry told his team. "You've got to wait for your opportunities and take advantage of them as they come."

The Cowboys went into the game a 3-point underdog, but the situation was far from bleak. While the Minnesota defense was rated as the best in the conference, their offensive was of a popgun variety, and they had gone through the entire season without a No.

1 quarterback. Gary Cuozzo, Norm Snead, and Bob Lee, who also served as the team's punter, shared the job.

Dallas got on the scoreboard quickly. After a Minnesota fumble gave the Cowboys the ball, Roger hit Bob Hayes running a down-and-in pattern on cornerback Ed Sharockman, the play netting 18 yards. Mike Clark came in to boot a 26-yard field goal.

The game then settled down to a duel between punters, with neither team showing much offensive strength. Roger was worrying because he was unable to move the team for long yardage, but he kept recalling what Landry had said over and over again during the week—to sit tight and wait for the opportunity. At halftime Dallas led, 6–3.

Late in the third quarter, the Cowboys launched a crucial scoring drive. It began when Charlie Waters was able to get some running room on a punt return and scamper 24 yards to the Dallas 48-yard line. On third down, with 15 yards needed for a first down, Staubach and Lance Alworth combined to victimize Sharockman. Alworth ran a turn-in pattern in front of Sharockman, one that reminded him of the one which Hayes had run in the first quarter when he had grabbed off the 18-yarder, but this time Alworth faked going deep, then suddenly stopped. Sharockman took the fake and kept going. Roger put the ball right in Alworth's hands. The play earned 29 yards and later would be cited as the "big play" of the afternoon. A minute or so later, the drive ended with Roger's 9-yard scoring pass to Bob Hayes. Now the game was out of the Vikings' reach. The final score was 20–12.

"We took their game away with our turnovers," said Landry after. Indeed it was true. Four Cowboy interceptions and a recovered fumble were significant. On the other hand, Roger's performance had been a flawless one. He had completed 10 passes in 14 tries, and not once had he been intercepted, not once had he or his teammates allowed a turnover of any type. "If they play like that for two more games, they'll be the world champions," said Minnesota quarterback Bob Lee.

The Cowboys now ranked as pro football's most formidable team, yet some people wondered whether their impeccable play was merely a prelude to their annual bubble-burst. Not Roger. There was not the slightest doubt in his mind that the team was going all the way—as long as he remained at quarterback.

After the Minnesota game, he pretended that he was disappointed with the way he and other Cowboys had performed. "This club," he said, shaking his head ominously, "is good for only two more games."

At the same time that the Cowboys were turning back the Vikings, the San Francisco 49ers were eliminating the Redskins from playoff competition. The two winners met on San Francisco's home grounds.

Roger was the game's hero. When he went back to pass and found the receivers double-covered, he'd run the ball, and the 49ers could do little to contain him. Roger galloped for a total of 55 yards, high for the day for the Dallas rushers.

On a drive in the fourth quarter that resulted in the clinching touchdown, Roger ran and passed for 3 big gains, setting up Duane Thomas' 1-yard burst for the touchdown.

It had been an incredible season for Roger. When it started, he had been fighting for a job. Not only had he unseated his rival, but he had managed to turn the Cowboys into consistent winners.

He had also been able to overhaul his image a bit. Many "experts," in their preseason estimates of the Cowboys, had said that Roger was a scrambler and that he had problems passing. Roger showed the fallacy of this by winning the NFL passing title and by winning it by the biggest margin in ten years. He accumulated a record of 8 points (4 points would have been perfect). Greg Landry, the second-place man, had 20 points. Roger led in the lowest percentage of interceptions (which earned him 1 point) and the longest average gain per pass (1 point), and he was second in completion percentage (2 points), and fourth in touchdown passes (4 points).

Roger also injected himself into the league's rushing statistics. He carried the ball 41 times for 343 yards, an average of 8.4 yards per carry, a higher percentage than anyone else in the league with 10 or more carries.

Another indication of Roger's advancement was a statement that Landry made. "I now recognize," he said, "the value of a quarterback being able to run." This didn't mean that he had accepted the run as sound football, only that he felt a running quarterback could play an important role. And that was progress.

The awards that document success cascaded into the Staubach home and Cowboy offices. These included:

The Bert Bell Award as the outstanding player in the NFL.

The *Sporting News* Player-of-the-Year Award.

118

The NFL's Offensive-Player-of-the-Year Award.

The Most-Valuable-Cowboy Award (voted by his teammates).

The Most-Popular Cowboy Award (voted by the fans).

Roger took the adulation in stride. It reminded him of the acclaim he had received after he won the Heisman Trophy. "He's so *different* from the kind of characters who have been popular the last few years," said Tex Schramm. "It kind of proves to me that the American public still wants an All-American type athlete to look up to."

Indeed, Roger spent little time dwelling upon what had been achieved; his mind was centered on what was yet to be accomplished. The idea that he had gone from a part-time quarterback to Player-of-the-Year in the space of a few months, and the fact that the Cowboys were NFC champions, neither of these would have any lasting significance, he knew, without a Super Bowl victory.

11 Super Game

The time: Sunday, January 16, 1972.
The place: Tulane Stadium, New Orleans.
The event: Super Bowl VI, the Dallas Cowboys vs. the Miami Dolphins.
At stake: The world professional football championship.

This time the Super Bowl had an added feature:

Running Roger vs. Bullet Bob, the "Bob," of course, being Miami quarterback Bob Griese. Many observers saw the contest as a duel between these two, the best young passers in professional football. Just as Staubach was the leading passer in the National Football Conference, so Griese was in the American Conference.

And Griese, like Staubach, could do more than throw. A onetime scrambler whose propensity to scramble had been curbed by Dolphin Coach Don Shula, Griese still liked to run the ball occasionally, but whereas Roger would gallop downfield for yardage, Griese was more inclined to run laterally to pass.

Staubach and Griese had much in common. Griese's wife, like Staubach's, was a former nurse. Staubach worked in real estate during off-season. So did Griese. Staubach was a college All American during his junior year. So was Griese—at Purdue.

Both grew up in the Midwest, Griese in Evansville, Indiana. Both were class presidents in high school, and, besides football, both starred in baseball and basketball. Both Catholics, they had wanted to go to Notre Dame. Both would wear No. 12 in pro football. "Modest" and "reserved" were two words often applied to each man.

Staubach was three years older than Griese, but both were born during the first week in February. Thus, as at least one astrologer noted, both were Aquarians. Anyone with the least bit of astrological awareness knows that Aquarians are supposed to be persons of great fixity of purpose when it comes to achieving established goals. That described Roger Staubach, all right. It also applied to Bob Griese.

Griese's path to pro football eminence had been much more direct than Roger's. A runner-up in the balloting for the Heisman Trophy, Griese was a first-draft choice of the Dolphins in 1967. The plan was for him to understudy John Stofa, the regular Miami quarterback, for at least a couple of seasons, but Stofa suffered a broken ankle in the first game of Griese's rookie season. Bob was sent in to fill the breach. The first few years were difficult. Griese suffered several painful injuries and the team lost many more games than it won.

Don Shula arrived upon the scene in 1970 and immediately turned things around. In 1969 the Dolphins won but 3 games; in 1970 they won 10. Of Griese, Shula once said: "Bob has a magnificent football brain. He is second to none in a huddle or on the line of scrimmage."

While there were a remarkable number of similarities about Staubach and Griese, there was one significant difference, and it was to have an important bearing on the game's outcome. It had to do with attitude, with the ability to adjust to the enormous pressure that builds in the two weeks preceding the Super Bowl. Roger had been through it before, even though he hadn't played. To Griese it was all new, all different.

"It's like no other game you ever play," Roger told Steve Perkins. What Roger meant was that it didn't follow the routine of the regular season—play a game, have a day off, practice for five days, and then you're

121

back in another game. With the Super Bowl, there's an extra week thrown in. "It's really tough on the nerves if you haven't been through it," Roger said.

The fact that players are away from home a full week also has its effect. During the regular season, when a team plays a road game players usually spend only one night in a hotel or motel, never more than two.

Then there's all the attention players receive. Well over a thousand press, radio, and television representatives cover the Super Bowl, and whenever a player leaves his hotel room, maybe just to buy a newspaper, he is confronted by people with notebooks, cameras, or microphones. It gets nerve-wracking.

The Dolphins had become champions of the Eastern Division of the AFC on the last day of the regular season by rallying to defeat the Green Bay Packers, while the same day, the Baltimore Colts, their closest rivals, were getting trimmed. In the conference play-offs against the Kansas City Chiefs, the Dolphins staggered through sixty minutes and the longest overtime period in football history before Garo Yepremian kicked the winning field goal. After that, beating the Colts in the AFC championship contest was no great problem.

Roger had been given so much information on the Dolphins that he felt he knew as much about the team as Don Shula. He may have.

The Cowboys were the first club to apply the science of electronic data processing to the business of evaluating opposing players and teams. What they were able to achieve was mind boggling.

The Dallas coaches and scouts screen films of an upcoming opponent, diagramming each play—both offense and defense—in each of several games. Formations, pass patterns, defensive sets (alignments), and adjustments, along with information as to the score, the down and distance, and the point in the game when the play occurred—all of this information and more is gleaned from the films and fed into a computer.

The computer takes the information, digests, categorizes it, and then on command spews out a two-hundred page report, filled with statistics, charts, and diagrams, a copy of which is distributed to each player and coach. Of course, it would be almost impossible for a player to be responsible for knowing all the report contains, so each man has to study only that part that applies to his position. Roger spent his time studying the Dolphins' defensive formations and tendencies. He wasn't concerned with what Bob Griese might do on a third-and-eight situation late in the third quarter with the Dolphins trailing by 9 points on an overcast day at Schaefer Stadium—but the information was probably there.

The scouting report that Roger was given on the Dolphins explained that the Miami defense was bulwarked by Nick Buoniconti, the team's quick and canny middle linebacker. At 5 feet 11, 220 pounds, Buoniconti was one of the smallest linebackers in pro football, but he made up for his lack of brawn with his seemingly intuitive knowledge of where a play was to go. His quickness and agility enabled him to get there. The "ready list" of plays that the Cowboys were to use in the game featured several counterplays that were meant to take advantage of Buoniconti's prescience. The idea of a counterplay is to get the opposition thinking that the play is going in one direction, then send the ballcarrier in the direction opposite. When Buoniconti reacted to what was really happening and cut back, a blocker would be there to cut him down. In practice sessions the week before the game, the Cowboys practiced counters over and over.

The scouting report also warned offense of Bill Stanfill, the Dolphins' 6-foot-5, 250-pound defensive right end, dangerous because of his talent in rushing the passer. A pro for only three years, Stanfill was already being labeled one of the surest tacklers in the game. He also had good speed and was capable of bringing runners down from behind. Left tackle Manny Fernandez was named another defensive standout. Few players were Fernandez's equal in determination and desire. To go along with these qualities, he had strength and quickness. He flew in on the pass rush and was the leading Dolphin in quarterback sacks. But, said the scouting report, Fernandez could be beaten on inside traps, that is, by luring him into a hole, then having a pulling lineman topple him from the side. There were trap plays on the ready list.

Both the scouting report and the game films that the team watched made it clear to Roger that he could not expect to throw the ball deep and expect to be successful against the Miami zone defense. Most of the players in the Miami secondary, including cornerbacks Curtis Johnson and Tim Foley and safety Jim Scott, were young and fast and reacted quickly. The same was true of the outside linebackers, Mike Kolen and

Doug Swift. All in all, Roger would be throwing into a defense that had good speed, was daring and aggressive.

Miami's defensive players were not well known and the press had labeled them the "no name defense." But the nickname could never be made to apply to the offensive unit, which had stars galore. The biggest names were Larry Csonka and Jim Kiick, the two bruising running backs who gave the Dolphins the most devasting running attack in pro football. Csonka, who had exceeded the magic 1,000-yard mark for the season, was especially brutal, the type of runner who broke tackles and could get 4 or 5 yards up the middle. Kiick, too, was the heavy-duty type, although he also had finely honed skills in catching the football. Frequently he was one of Griese's targets.

Paul Warfield was being hailed as the game's premier pass receiver. He had come to the Dolphins in a preseason trade with the Cleveland Browns, where he had established himself as being of All Pro caliber. As Warfield raced downfield, he moved so effortlessly he seemed to be gliding. He had the necessary moves to get loose in heavy traffic, and his speed made him a constant deep threat.

Warfield's name became well known a few days before the game. President Nixon called Don Shula to wish him luck and, in the course of the conversation, he told him, "The down-and-in pass to Warfield ought to work against Dallas." Newspapers across the country carried a diagram of the President's play, and it showed Warfield going straight downfield for about 10 yards, then angling toward the middle of the field.

125

President Johnson was an ally of the Cowboys. Just before the team left for New Orleans, Landry was handed a telegram that read: "My prayers and my presence will be with you in New Orleans—although I have no plans to send any plays. Lyndon B. Johnson."

"Well," said Landry, "at least we have one President on our side."

In contrast to the Cowboys and their multiple offense, the Miami attack was uncomplicated. As one coach observed, "The Dolphins kept it simple. It's almost as if they handed out their plays to the opposition and said, 'This is what we do—you try and stop us.'"

The Cowboys stayed at the Hilton Inn, about a half hour's drive from the downtown area, while the Dolphins were quartered at the Fontainebleau, only a few minutes from the French Quarter and Bourbon Street, the nightclub section of the city. While the Hilton was less frantic than where the Dolphins were staying, it had the disadvantage of being close to the airport, and at night the scream of jet aircraft landing and taking off caused many players to lose sleep.

Roger hardly left the motel. He spent so much time in his room screening films, even having room service bring him his meals, that one reporter said he was becoming a hermit. Roger protested. "I've been out," he said. "I went to the French Quarter once, for some shrimp.

"New Orleans is a great place to visit, that is, if you have nothing on your mind. But the game on Sunday is what it is all about to us. I've got to keep thinking in that direction."

Super Sunday was sun-filled but chilly. The temperature never got as high as forty degrees. As the fans—81,023 of them—crowded their way into Tulane Stadium, the pregame show got under way. It was kind of gridiron Mardi Gras, featuring a dozen college marching bands and blaring music, more than two hundred parading girls, soaring balloons and flying pigeons. Roger, concentrating on warming up, hardly noticed.

The Cowboys stood in a line, their heads erect, as "The Star-Spangled Banner" was played. Roger, as usual, stood ramrod straight, as if he were on the parade grounds at the Naval Academy.

Mike Clark kicked off, sailing the ball to the Miami 6-yard line. There fleet Mercury Morris gathered it in and hurried to the 26. Griese was unable to move the team, and after the punt the Cowboys took over on their own 21.

The first play from scrimmage worked just the way that Landry had diagrammed it, with Roger hitting Bob Hayes on the right flat. It got the Cowboys 5 yards. Then Duane Thomas charged through the left side of the Miami line for this first down.

But Roger did not look nearly as sharp on the next series. On the first down he was unable to find a receiver, and Manny Fernandez knifed through to bring him down for a 6-yard loss. On the next play, another pass, Roger was indecisive again. This time he ended up running with the ball and gained a yard up the middle. He had a chance to make amends on third down when Lance Alworth got free on a sideline pattern. Roger let loose and the ball sailed way over Alworth's head. He couldn't have gotten it with a stepladder. When Roger trotted off the field, his fists were clenched and his chin was on his chest.

The next time the Cowboys got the ball, Roger again had trouble reading the Dolphins' zone coverage. So he did what he felt he had to do—run with the ball. One of his scrambles earned the Cowboys a first down on the Miami 45. Now Landry began sending in the counterplays that the Cowboys had drilled on, and they worked to perfection. Garrison got 8 yards off right guard, and then 10 yards, again through the right side.

Roger worked the team closer and closer to the Miami end zone. But inside the 10-yard line, the Miami line toughened. With its first down on the 7, the Dolphins stopped Thomas and then Garrison, and then Thomas a second time after he had caught a screen pass. Mike Clark came in to boot a field goal and send the Cowboys into a 3–0 lead.

Roger had shown that he was beginning to settle down, to assume command. But Griese was having problems. Late in the first quarter, he called a down-and-in pattern to Paul Warfield—"the President's play" —but Mel Renfro was there to break it up. On the next play, Griese darted back to throw again. No one was open. He went back some more. In charged Bob Lilly. Griese turned and ran and Lilly pursued him. Larry Cole joined in the chase. Griese dodged desperately to the right, then to the left. Suddenly Lilly lunged, caught hold, and crumpled the white-shirted

Dolphin quarterback to the ground. The crowd gasped; the play had lost 29 yards. Griese was never the same after that.

The Cowboys were unable to take advantage of Miami's mistakes until six minutes before halftime. Roger passed to Duane Thomas for one first down, and then pitched out to Thomas for another.

Now it was second-and-nine on the Dallas 47. Landry sent in a pass play. Mike Ditka was to be the primary receiver. The big, brawny tight end was to sprint 10 yards downfield, then cut. At this point, he would be in between Miami's zones of coverage, and Roger was to hit him with a short, quick throw. If it worked, it would get the Cowboys a first down and keep their drive going.

Roger got the snap and darted back. When he planted his right foot and drew back his arm to throw, Ditka was right where he was supposed to be. But Nick Buoniconti had diagnosed the play and dropped back with Ditka, and he was covering the Dallas receiver like a coat of paint. Roger could have run. Later, looking at the films, the coaches might have said a run was warranted. But out of the corner of his eye, Staubach caught a glimpse of Lance Alworth, his secondary receiver.

Alworth had lined up on the left side and broken straight downfield at the snap. Now, as he veered across the middle, Staubach could see that he had beaten the man covering him by a full step. Roger drilled the ball home. The wiry Alworth grabbed it, his teeth tightly clenched, bracing for the hit, and then he

129

struggled several more yards before the Dolphins could bring him down.

It was, as Roger was to say after, "a turning-point play." It took the Cowboys 21 yards to the Miami 32.

Now Roger went back to the ground attack, again using counters. Calvin Hill ripped through Nick Buoniconti's territory for 13 yards. Hill went for 7 more, then for 5 yards on a reverse, a good call. Not much more than a minute remained in the first half. The crowd was on its feet and screaming.

Roger needed only seconds. From the 7-yard line, he pedaled back, then quickly rifled the ball to Alworth in the corner where the goal line meets the sideline. *Touchdown!* Clark's kick made it 10–0.

In the closing seconds of the second period, the Dolphins managed to get onto the scoreboard when Garo Yepremian kicked a 31-yard field goal. But Miami's hopes of overcoming the Cowboys' 7-point lead were dashed the first time the Cowboys got possession in the third period.

Landry called for a change in strategy. The Cowboys had been running up the middle; now they began going wide. Thomas took a pitchout and swept for 4 yards and a first down on the Dallas 32. Two more sweeps followed Roger's pass to Calvin Hill, putting the Cowboys deep in Miami territory once more.

On first down at the Dolphin 6, Roger sent Garrison around the left side, and he picked up 3 yards. The Cowboys huddled, waiting silently for Landry's messenger. The play sent in was a rollout, with Roger to drift to the weak side and either pass or run, depending on how the defense reacted. But when the team broke from the huddle, Roger noticed that the Dolphins were in a standard defense, not the goal line defense that the Landry play was meant to exploit. So Roger checked off, calling a pitchout to Duane Thomas. It worked—Thomas cutting to his left, then veering into the end zone. That was the clincher. It made the score 17–3—and a two touchdown lead was insurmountable the way the Dallas defense was playing.

Indeed, the Dolphins did not come close to getting a touchdown. In the fourth period, Chuck Howley intercepted a pass meant for Jim Kiick, and he ran it back 41 yards to the Miami 9-yard line. Three plays later Roger connected with tight end Mike Ditka for the touchdown. After Clark's kick, the score was 23–3. And that is how it ended.

At the final gun, Rayfield Wright and Ditka hauled Landry onto their shoulders and rode him off the field. Roger could hear their shouts of joy and see the happiness in Landry's eyes. He saw Bob Lilly jump high in the air in exultation. He remembered the Super Bowl defeat of the year before and how Lilly had thrown his helmet across the field when the Colts kicked their last-ditch field goal. Enthusiastic Dallas fans were pouring onto the field and the players had to fight their way to the runway leading to the locker room.

It was a madhouse inside. Players and writers were jammed together under the hot glare of television lights. TV men with cameras mounted on their shoulders tried to focus on interviews that were being conducted from an elevated platform that had been erected in one corner of the room.

The biggest mob of all surrounded Staubach's locker.

As Roger peeled off his uniform, several reporters asked him to cite the game's turning points. He thought for a second. "There were two that I recall," he said. "Larry Csonka fumbled in the first quarter when Miami had a good drive going. That was one.

"Another was the pass that I completed to Lance Alworth late in the second quarter. He was the secondary receiver, but Mike Ditka, the tight end, was covered.

"After Alworth's catch, we went in to score. That made the score ten to nothing. We had taken control."

Someone gave Roger the news that he had been voted the game's most valuable player and, as such, would receive a sports car from *Sport* magazine. Roger flashed a grin. "I'm really surprised," he said. "That's great! We've got three girls and a new car will come in handy."

Then he grew more serious. "That's the way it is in this business," he said. "When the team does good, the quarterback gets the credit. I'll take it; I'm not turning it down, but there are an awful lot of guys who should be in for a share."

The game's statistics showed that Roger completed 12 of 19 passes for 119 yards without an interception. He ran with the ball 5 times, gaining 18 yards. In total, the Cowboys gained 252 yards on the ground, a Super Bowl record.

That, to Roger, was the game's most significant statistic. "When you're running like that," he told reporters, "the passing has to open up."

He revealed that he had been hit hard twice. Once in the third quarter when he went back to pass and the Dolphins' Jake Scott leveled him on a safety blitz. "I saw him coming," Roger said. "But there was nothing I could do. He forced me to release the ball sooner than I wanted to. Bob Hayes was open on the play, but I missed."

A reporter recalled that Staubach had staggered to the sidelines. "The breath was knocked out of me and my ribs hurt," Roger said. "But after I got my wind back, I was OK."

Then he added with a grin, "That's what I get for staying in the pocket."

One by one, the Dallas players came over to Roger's locker, wedged their way through the crowd, and shook Roger's hand or clapped him on the back. George Andrie was one. "You always told us," said Andrie, " 'Let's lift one more for the Super Bowl.' "

"What did he mean by that?" a reporter wanted to know.

Roger explained: "At the end of our weightlifting sessions during the off-season, I'd always say, 'I'm going to take you to the Super Bowl. Let's lift one more for the Super Bowl.' George was just reminding me of that."

As the crowd in the dressing room began to thin out, Roger buttoned a knit shirt and pulled on a navy-blue windbreaker. Hundreds of fans were gathered outside of the dressing room exit, held back by police barriers. When they saw Roger they cheered and then began to serenade him with a chorus of "Anchors Aweigh." Roger, smiling, waved a thank you. It was the perfect ending.

12 Priorities

This is around noontime on Friday, July 28, 1972. The All Star Football Game, the champion Dallas Cowboys vs. the College All Stars, will be played at Soldier Field at eight o'clock. The scene now is the Grand Ballroom of the Conrad Hilton Hotel in Chicago, where a luncheon sponsored by the Fellowship of Christian Athletes is just getting under way.

More than a thousand high school athletes, representing what local people like to call "Chicagoland," are on hand. Among those seated on the dais are Tom Osborne, an assistant coach at the University of Nebraska, Dallas Coach Tom Landry, and Roger Staubach. Now it's Roger's turn to speak.

"I believe in God," he begins.

"I believe in the Son of God, Jesus Christ.

"I believe in His Plan.

"I try to lead the type of life He would want."

Football is important to Roger Staubach. Very important. But there are several other things in his life that outrank it in importance. His religion is one. His family is another.

It perplexes Roger that so few people talk about God today. "You mention God," he says, "and they put a halo on you or label you a square or fanatic. That's not right.

"Reasoning powers should tell you that there is something higher in the universe. Life would be insignificant without a relationship to God."

Roger keeps very active with the Fellowship of Christian Athletes, an interdenominational, interracial organization that every reader of the sports pages has heard about. The purpose of the FCA is "to confront athletes and coaches, and through them the youth of the nation, with the challenge and adventure of following Christ and serving Him. . . ."

The FCA arranges for such confrontations by sending teams of athletes, coaches and other interested adults to conferences and rallies in high schools and on college campuses. In addition, the organization holds a score or more of annual national conferences which stress athletic development and spiritual growth for high school and college athletes and coaches.

Who are some of the pro football players involved in the FCA program? Daryle Lamonica, quarterback for the Oakland Raiders; Ted Kwalick, tight end for the San Francisco 49ers; Winston Hill, tackle for the New York Jets; Ray Nitschke, linebacker for the Green Bay Packers; Fran Tarkenton, quarterback for the Minnesota Vikings; and Tim Foley, defensive back for the Miami Dolphins.

A handful of Roger's Cowboy teammates are also members of the Fellowship of Christian Athletes and are not reluctant to speak out as he does. Or as Tom

Landry does. Among them are Dan Reeves, Walt Garrison, Billy Truax, and Calvin Hill. Some other members of the Dallas team shun such activity. They're known as Swingers. Roger and his band are called, privately, at least, the Christers. The two groups mesh without any problems on the playing field. Off the field, however, the members of one group see little of the other.

"The FCA uses us because we are popular," says Roger. "To some students, we're heroes. So we can serve as a vehicle to get young people to know Christ and be better persons for it."

But understand this, Roger is no crusader, no evangelist. "I'm not trying to convert anyone," he says. "I'm not saying, 'Hey, you should live the kind of life that I do.' I just try to influence young people by telling them how to live. Let them take it from there."

The FCA dates to 1947, the year that a young Oklahoma coach gave a talk that was titled, "Making My Vocation Christian." The basic idea upon which the FCA was founded was contained in that address. Several years later, baseball's Branch Rickey, then general manager of the Pittsburgh Pirates, and several Pittsburgh businessmen provided the organization with enough financial support to get it started.

In recent years, the FCA has shown remarkable growth. About ten thousand athletes attended the national conferences each year. There are now one thousand five hundred FCA groups across the country, and more than two hundred cities have active FCA chapters.

To see Roger address an FCA meeting is a moving

experience. If the letter carrier on your route or a local bus driver confessed to you of his belief in God, and his burning desire to do His will, you would be impressed by the man's sincerity, stirred by his ability to tell you what was in his heart. When Roger Staubach or any other "name" athlete does this, young people are deeply impressed, deeply stirred.

The audience listens intently as Roger begins to speak. The room grows silent. He speaks calmly, evenly, never raising his voice. The words seem to come from deep within him, and it is as if he is reaching out and touching every person in the room.

Roger often speaks of his faith in terms of football strategy. During ceremonies in Cincinnati on Roger Staubach Day in 1972, he said, "In football, the defense is the best friend of the offense because the defense provides you with good field position. Then it's up to you, the offense, to get across the goal line, and it's up to me, the quarterback, to motivate the team.

"In this world everyone has a good 'field position' to start out with, because God has placed us on earth. If you've been created you've got somewhere to go, a final 'goal line' to cross–salvation. Faith is critical for you to reach the goal."

While Roger is a Catholic and applauds the stand of the Catholic Church on moral issues, he feels that one's particular religious affiliation is less important than, as he puts it, "what's inside you—your acceptance of Christ." He says, "I'm a Catholic because I still have the concept that the Catholic Church is the Church established by Christ, and my goal is to be with Christ in His eternal life. But I think that Protestants and all Christians will reach the same goal as I'm seeking if they accept Christ into their lives.

"If I were a Jewish man, I'd have a love of God and a concept of how he'd want me to live my life. I'd have a respect for Christ, whereas in my case I believe in Christ as Our Saviour."

How does Roger feel about athletes, pro football quarterbacks, in particular, whose life-style features blondes, brunettes, and Johnny Walker Red? "Someone like that," says Roger, "should sit back and mind his own business—not go around telling people that this free-living and free-loving way is right. He shouldn't be writing books or magazine articles about it.

"But I don't believe that just because you're an athlete you should try and be an example or say things you don't believe. That's hypocrisy."

Roger has been criticized for mouthing pious phrases while at the same time making a career out of a sport that puts an emphasis on violence and brutality. "Football is not violent," says Roger in answer to such criticism. "When I think of violence, I think of guns, crime, and beatings.

"Football is *physical*," he says. "Every time I get in my car, I have a better chance of being involved in something violent than I do when I get out on the football field.

"If I thought football was violent, I wouldn't be playing it. I'm just a skinny little guy trying to use my talents."

Life has a way, Roger likes to point out, of drilling home to us what's important and what isn't. He recalls a winter afternoon during the off-season one year when he visited a hospital to show film of football highlights to a nine-year-old boy who was dying of leukemia. Roger met the boy, chatted with him, and screened the film. But Roger was in a hurry; he had to get back downtown to buy a suit. As he was leaving the hospital, Roger was told that the boy was not expected to live through the weekend. "Suddenly," Roger recalls, "buying a suit didn't seem very important anymore.

"People are important, not things. That boy died two days later.

"Next to my belief in God," says Roger, "I center my life around my family. I believe in the family strongly. It is critical and essential to my life and me. That's what life is all about."

These are Roger's words from a speech he delivered in June, 1972, after being named "Sports Father of the Year." At the time, Roger's family included his wife, Marianne; Jennifer, a chatty six-year-old; Michelle, four and quiet; and Stephanie, two.

Not long ago, Roger, Marianne, and their three young daughters were happily looking forward to the birth of the fourth Staubach child. Roger tells what happened: "During the delivery, something went wrong. The baby girl was stillborn."

To Roger, the tragedy was a test. "Why me, Lord?" —that was the question that he felt compelled to ask. "It wasn't a long rebellion," Roger said in an article in *Guideposts.* "I prayed for understanding, and when I did I felt this sudden sense of peace and comfort."

The Staubachs live in a ranch-style brick house of modest size in the Dallas suburb of Richardson. Roger's wife drives the station wagon awarded him as the Super Bowl MVP. (He was originally given a sports car, but he explained to *Sport* magazine that if it didn't make any difference, he would just as soon have a station wagon. He was, after all, a family man and needed extra space for kids, strollers, playpens, diaper bags, picnic baskets, etc.) Roger's three young daughters used to use his NFL Player-of-the-Year trophy and other large trophies as hobbyhorses. Often Roger throws passes to neighborhood youngsters. No letter of request for an autograph ever goes unanswered.

Visit the Staubach home and you see Roger's ideas about the family reflected in the decor. Posters proclaiming love and peace adorn the living-room walls. So do the children's drawings, even Stephanie's scribbles.

"Living in a family is a real lesson in life," Roger has said. "It teaches you things like love, respect, understanding, and the meaning of sharing."

Roger has often said that a parent's primary responsibility is to be an example to his children. "It's easy to tell the children the ideal way to do things, but if I don't live that way and do those things, they won't either."

The best way to show children how to live, says Roger, is to focus your life on Christ. "He is the best example there is of love, understanding, and sharing."

Roger and his wife stress togetherness in their family life. On weekends during the off-season, they often take the children swimming or picnicking.

Even when the girls were very young, Marianne would take them to see Dallas home games occasionally. They'd watch for Roger's number or listen for his name.

Roger and Marianne share the role of family disciplinarian, but like virtually all parents they have doubts about what they may or may not be achieving. "I believe in strictness, but to what degree, I don't quite know," says Roger. "You have to weigh all the circumstances of the situation and then decide what you think is the best approach. We'll find out in six or seven years if we're doing a good job."

Roger is also active in crusading against drug use on the part of young people. Roger says that the boy or girl who is courageous—and really "cool"—is the one who says "no" to drugs.

"The associations you make now will affect your career and entire adult life," Roger tells youth groups. "If your crowd or your friends are on drugs, you only have two choices. Either you've got to be for drugs so strongly that you don't care what you do with your life, or else you've got to be against them so strongly that you'll work to get your best friend off drugs—or completely drop your friend or your group."

"What about drug abuse in the ranks of pro football players?" Roger is sometimes asked.

"They are being used, to what extent I don't know," he says. "Probably in the same proportion as among businessmen or housewives or any other groups in our society.

"I don't know why anyone should want to use drugs. They're just a crutch. Unfortunately, when athletes use them, they get all the publicity. Housewives and businessmen don't."

After the Cowboys' Super Bowl victory, Roger was inundated with requests for personal appearances. Some involved very large fees; others were requests from groups and organizations of a religious or fund-raising nature. These frequently offered only a token fee or none at all.

Roger's first impulse was to make those speeches that he felt would accomplish the most good. The matter of payment was incidental. Curt Mosher, public relations manager of the Cowboys, shook his head in wonderment. "He has to be protected from his own good intentions," said Mosher. "He's the easiest touch in the world for a speaking engagement." Finally, Roger agreed to a compromise. For every paid appearance Roger made, he accepted one for nothing.

Roger also decided to limit to three or four his associations with commercial firms. One contract he did sign was with the Aurora Plastics Company, a toy manufacturer ("Skittle Bowl," Skittle Pool," etc.), and he agreed to make appearances at toy fairs and trade shows for the firm. He also signed on as a part-time athletic director of a summer camp for boys, and he continued to be listed as a staff member of a Dallas real estate firm.

What did winning the Super Bowl mean to Roger Staubach? The personal recognition was nice, and he had no idea of refusing the $15,000 he earned as a member of the winning team. But what really counted was the idea of having accomplished something, of having set a goal and achieved it.

Roger himself did the negotiating when he signed a new contract with the Cowboys early in 1973. It guaranteed him about $75,000 a year for three years. "It's not the highest price ever paid a quarterback," he said. "But I'm satisfied."

As these paragraphs imply, Roger took the rewards and riches that followed the Super Bowl win very much in stride. One reason is that he realizes that fame is very fleeting. He likes to recall an incident that took place after he had returned from Vietnam and near the end of his long stay at the Pensacola Naval Air Station. He was asked to speak to a group of business-men in Anniston, Alabama. On the day he was to give the address, Roger drove north to Anniston, and when he arrived at the site of the meeting, the local Holiday Inn, a big sign in front proclaimed: WELCOME TO ANNISTON, ROGER STEINBECK. And when he got up to speak, that's the way he was introduced. Athletic fame, says Roger, is "temporary hoopla."

But there's another reason that Roger is unaffected by the acclaim he's received. "That there are more important things in life than football," he has said many times. "We are here for something greater than the Super Bowl."

13 Star-Crossed Season

It would be nice to end the Roger Staubach story right after Super Bowl VI. He is leaving Tulane Stadium as the game's Most Valuable Player, the man who has led the Dallas Cowboys to the promised land—finally. The crowd cheers. The strains of "Anchors Away" are heard in the background. Marianne rushes up and kisses him. They walk off together. *Music up and out. Roll credits. End.*

Life isn't like that. It's especially not like that for Roger Staubach.

Roger's greatest triumphs have frequently been followed by cheerless periods. After winning a scholarship to the Naval Academy, he flunked the entrance examination. He captured the Heisman Trophy as the greatest college player, then was ambushed in the Cotton Bowl. Three lovely daughters, then a stillborn child.

In 1971 Roger had the kind of season every pro player dreams about. But 1972 was a nightmare.

Roger didn't have much time to celebrate the Super Bowl victory. A week later he was starting quarterback and co-captain for the NFC All Stars when they faced the AFC squad in the Pro Bowl.

During one of the Pro Bowl practice sessions, Roger met Greg Landry. The Detroit quarterback noticed that Roger was wearing especially small shoulder pads.

"The way you run," said Landry, "you've got to be crazy to wear those things." Roger explained that larger pads would serve to reduce his mobility. He shrugged off the warning.

Roger had much more to be concerned about than his shoulder pads that afternoon. He had the opportunity to call his own plays, and did so. But time after time he was thrown for losses. He never got one sustained drive going and he threw two costly interceptions.

The game was a disappointment for Roger. Any failure is. But this defeat, coming so soon on the heels of that heady day in New Orleans, was especially frustrating.

"It brought me back to earth, and in that way it was good for me," said Roger after. "I came away from it determined to work hard during the off-season, and be sure I was really prepared for training camp."

Before the 1972 season got under way, *Sport* magazine sent ballots to the NFL players asking them to select the top teams and the men they felt would win individual honors in each conference during the upcoming season. Roger had to be gladdened by the results. The players forecast that Roger would be picked as the most valuable player in the National Football Conference. As for the conference's top passer, they rated Roger second only to John Brodie of the 49ers. The Cowboys were chosen to repeat in the Super Bowl by an overwhelming margin of ballots.

During training camp, Staubach and Morton were interviewed about the future. Both made references to the hazards of being a pro quarterback.

"I'm looking forward to a lot of good seasons," said Roger, then added, "if I don't get into an injury situation."

Morton said this: "I think for the Cowboys to continue to be a great football team it is going to take both Roger and myself. I just can't see one quarterback going the whole year, not the way the game is now.

"The last few years we've been playing twenty-three or twenty-four games. Anything can happen."

"Anything" began happening in the very first game

of the exhibition season, the Cowboys vs. the College All Stars at Soldier Field in Chicago. Roger was shaken up when running the ball in the second quarter. The fact that his head was hurting him didn't bother him as much as the fact that he couldn't think clearly. "I just went completely blank," he was to say.

In came Craig Morton to pitch the Cowboys to a 20–7 win. By the fourth quarter, Roger's mind was clear again and he probably could have gone back in, but Landry kept him on the sidelines.

Roger continued to do a good deal of running in the exhibition games that followed. The Cowboys' pass offense was slow in coming around, so Roger relied on his runs to keep drives going.

The Cowboys were also having trouble scoring once they had gotten inside the 10-yard line. Roger was determined to overcome this failing. In a preseason game against the Rams in Los Angeles, the Cowboys were within striking distance of the goal line.

Roger took the ball and skirted an end. He had 3 yards to go for a touchdown at the end of a 9-yard gallop when suddenly linebacker Marlin McKeever, who outweighed Roger by forty pounds, loomed in his path. Roger was near the sideline and could easily have stepped out of bounds. Fran Tarkenton would have. Greg Landry would have. But Roger tried to cut inside McKeever. No way; McKeever had the angle. When he struck, there was a loud *thwack*. Roger went down, his face contorted in pain. He knew immediately that he had been hurt—and he was right. After examining him in the locker room, they gave

146

him the bad news. He had suffered a shoulder separation.

The next day, back in Dallas, they operated on Roger, pinning his shoulder back together, and they told him that it would be eight to twelve weeks before he would be able to play again.

"Tough luck, Roger," everyone said to him. "Too bad." But he knew what they wanted to say, that if he had been a pocket-style quarterback it never would have happened. He knew that deep down everyone was thinking, "I told you so."

Despite the injury and the fact that he would be sidelined for almost all of the season, Roger gave no thought to abandoning his style of play. "I'm still going to play the way I play," he said. "I'm going to run with the ball.

"Running is a good thing when it's done right. If I knew it didn't help the team, I'd stop. It really hurts the defense and I think it helps the offensive linemen."

Roger did agree to make one concession, however— he would wear bigger shoulder pads, the type running backs wear.

One gloomy day followed another. He had looked forward eagerly to the season because he had wanted to prove his consistency, to demonstrate that he had the ability to win games over more than one season. Now he didn't even have his job. He was right back where he had been more than a year before.

Sad and pale, his right arm in a tight sling, Roger watched as Craig Morton directed the Cowboys to a 10-4 record, good enough to earn the team a berth in the championship playoffs.

By mid-October Roger was throwing the ball again. Landry began using him in games late in the season, but only after the contest was out of danger or hopelessly lost. Morton was the Cowboy quarterback, Roger the backup man again.

Roger's brief appearance did not win him any acclaim. "He's still rusty," said Landry as the playoff games drew near. "He's having trouble finding his receivers.

"But," Landry added, "we'll play him if we need him."

The day came when the Cowboys needed Roger, really needed him. In the playoff game against the San Francisco 49ers, the Cowboys trailed, 28–13, with less than two minutes remaining in the third period. Landry, seeking to change the mood of the game, sent Staubach in as Morton's replacement.

Roger fumbled. He missed some passes. On the 49ers' side of the field players began clapping one another on the back. San Francisco linebacker Dave Wilcox peered across the line of scrimmage and shouted out to the Super Bowl champions, "Hey, you guys! How docs it feel losing?"

Then Calvin Hill broke loose on a long run to set up a Cowboy field goal. Dallas now trailed by 12 points. But it was getting very late; less than two minutes remained.

Suddenly Roger caught fire. He connected on three straight passes, giving the Cowboys a first down on the San Francisco 20-yard line.

"I think the post pattern to Parks will be open," Landry said to Roger during a time-out. Roger agreed.

Parks got a step on the cornerback, and when he did, the ball was there.

Now it was 28–23. One minute, six seconds were left.

The Cowboys' only hope was an outside kick. Tony Fritsch approached the ball at normal speed but tapped it to the right, and it caromed off a San Francisco player to be recovered for the Cowboys by Mel Renfro. The San Francisco fans sat in stunned silence, hardly believing what was unfolding down below.

First down for Dallas at midfield. Roger scampered back to throw, saw an opening up the middle and took off. Twenty-one yards! A first down on the San Francisco 29-yard line. Roger then connected with Billy Parks on a sideline pattern, and Parks was run out of bounds on the 10-yard line.

In the huddle, Ron Sellers, who was playing tight end, said to Roger: "They're taking the outside away from me. I can beat my man." Roger fired a perfect pass over the middle and Sellers grabbed it for the touchdown. Dallas—incredibly—had won.

"I can't believe it," Ron Sellers kept saying on the way to the locker room. "I can't believe it."

Neither could the 49ers. Neither could the fans. Nobody could.

The Cowboy locker room was wild with excitement. Players, coaches, and even Landry were jumping up and down and screaming. "I've never been this excited," said Landry. "I've never seen us so emotional. I guess we weren't this emotional after the Super Bowl because we could see it coming.

"This one kind of . . . well, burst on us."

Although Roger was the man of the hour, he was less exultant than the others. "I'm just glad I could contribute," he said. "I hadn't really contributed anything all season and I'm glad I could.

"Craig Morton could have done the same thing. He got some bad breaks in there, but he could have turned it around, too."

The game has to rank as one of the most dramatic victories in Cowboy history. Yet the memory of the contest has all but been blotted out. That's because of what happened the very next week in the Conference championship match against the Redskins at RFK Stadium in Washington.

The question of who would be the Dallas starting quarterback was debated all week long in the press. But Landry really had no choice. The fans realized that there would have been no game with the Redskins if Roger had not come off the bench to work his miracle. If Landry had not permitted him to start, surely the coach's life would have been in jeopardy.

Early in the game, the Redskins found a weakness in the Cowboy secondary and they exploited it to the fullest, specifically, with a pair of long touchdown passes from Bill Kilmer to Charlie Taylor. The Redskin defense, meanwhile, throttled down the Dallas running game. Roger, with 59 yards in 5 carries, outgained Calvin Hill and Walt Garrison combined.

The final score showed the Redskins on top, 26–3. "They just beat the hell out of us," said a dejected Bob Lilly afterward. "Just beat the hell out of us."

Roger took the loss as a personal calamity. Never before had the Cowboy team been beaten in a game that Roger had started and finished. A Dallas sports-writer who visited the locker room after the game described Roger as "looking as though he had just lost his country, his family and his friends."

"We just couldn't make the third-down plays," Roger lamented. "We missed three of them by about a foot." True; the Cowboys got first downs only 3 times on 12 attempts in third-down situations.

While the defeat was very hard for Roger to take, some of the postgame criticism hurt just as much.

A few of the Redskin players said that they were glad Roger had started the game instead of Morton. "They had the wrong man in there," said Washington defensive tackle Diron Talbert. "We were glad to see Staubach. He was rusty and couldn't find his receivers."

Roger called the statement "bush league," adding, "A real team wouldn't have made a statement after the fact."

Yet Roger feels personally responsible for what happened that gray afternoon in Washington. "I was supposed to come up with the big plays and I didn't," he says. "We tried grinding it out and we couldn't. I should have come up with something else.

"I want to come back and make up for the mess."

Roger and the Cowboys came close to redeeming themselves the very next season. But they fell one step short.

Roger ended up as the league's leading passer once more, while the team finished with a 10-4 record and moved into the NFC title game for the fourth straight season by downing the Los Angeles Rams in the first of the play-off contests.

One play in that game must be recounted. The Cowboys built a 17-0 lead but the Rams came back to narrow the margin, 17-16. Play was in the fourth quarter, Dallas' ball, third and 14 on their own 17. In came the play from Coach Landry, a pass with rookie Drew Pearson to be the primary receiver.

Roger agreed that the play had to be a pass. But instead of merely trying for a first down, he decided to take the Ram defense by surprise and go for the touchdown. In the huddle he changed Pearson's route, assigning him to fly for the Ram end zone. Landry had wanted him to run a turn-in pattern.

As Roger dropped back to throw, he saw the Ram zone begin to form, with safety Steve Peerce slanting over to pickup Pearson. Roger drew the ball back and pump-faked. Peerce took the fake and Pearson sprinted right by him. Then Roger did throw. Pearson fought off another defender to make the catch at the 50, and from there it was clear sailing to the goalline. The shocked Rams were never able to recover.

One other play in the game was critical, one in which Calvin Hill suffered a dislocated elbow. Hill had turned in a brilliant season, rushing for a total of 1,142 yards and averaging 4.2 yards per carry. But he was on the sidelines the next week when the Cowboys met the Minnesota Vikings for the Conference championship. Superstar Bob Lilly was another injury victim that afternoon. Combine this bad fortune with the fact that Roger did not have one of his better days, and it is not difficult to understand how the potent Vikings were able to outplay and outpoint the Cowboys. Roger watched the Super Bowl on television again.

What's ahead for Roger Staubach? What are his goals?

"I'd like to play until I'm thirty-eight," he has said. "I think I'll still be able to do a good job then. I feel I'll be in better condition than the usual thirty-year-old quarterback because of the years I spent in the Navy."

He explains his thinking thusly: If a quarterback plays from age twenty-two to thirty-eight, it means that he has taken sixteen years of punishment. But Roger, at thirty-eight, would have had played only ten years. "I'd be the age of a thirty-two-year-old quarterback at thirty-eight, from the standpoint of physical beatings."

The logic here is open to question. But there is one facet of Roger's grand plan that cannot be doubted, and that is his will, his desire. He wants to be recognized as the best quarterback in professional football. If that is what he wants, it's likely he will achieve it.

Roger Staubach has been a winner all his life—in high school, at the Naval Academy, and in pro football. He will be again. Anyone who knows him says so.

INDEX

Adderley, Herb, 10, 95
All Star games, 56–58, 134, 146
Allen, Ermal, 89
Allen, George, 69, 92, 97
Alworth, Lance, 10, 94, 106–8, 111, 116, 128–29, 132
American Football Conference, 9, 122
American Football League, 56
Andrie, George, 13, 94, 133
Appleton, Scott, 50, 53
Army-Navy games, 37–43, 48
Aurora Plastics Company, 142

Baker, Ralph, 76
Balaban, Tom, 20
Baltimore Colts, 77, 88, 122
Bancroft Hall (Annapolis), 29–30, 38–39
Beathard, Pete, 49
Belden, Bob, 74
Bell, Bobby, 35
Bellino, Joe, 25, 55
Berry, Ray, 67
Blanda, George, 80
Borden, Paul, 58–59
Bradley, Bill, 95
Brandt, Gil, 61–62
Brinkman, Eddie, 21
Brodie, John, 13, 88
Brown, Larry, 98
Buffalo Bills, 95
Buffone, Doug, 102
Buoniconti, Nick, 123–24, 129–30

Carlisle, Duke, 51
Carnevale, Ben, 43–44
Chicago Bears, 101–3
Clark, Mike, 13, 98, 108, 116, 127, 130–31
Cleveland Browns, 56, 71
Cole, Larry, 94, 128
Corum, Gene, 45
Cosell, Howard, 98
Cotton Bowl game, 1964, 49–53
Csonka, Larry, 125, 132
Cuozzo, Gary, 116

Dallas Cowboys, 9, 11–15, 57–59, 61, 64, 66–70; All Star game, 134; Eastern Division champions, 115; Electronic scouting, 122–24; Seasons: 1968, 70–72; 1969, 83–86; 1970, 86–88; 1971, 90–115; 1972, 144–53; Super Bowl, 119–33
Defensive strategy, 77–82
Detroit Lions, 88, 92
Dietzel, Paul, 37–38, 41
Ditka, Mike, 10, 14, 95, 98, 102, 107, 109, 129, 131–32
Donnelly, Pat, 46, 50, 52
Duden, Dick, 34

Edwards, Dave, 10, 94
Edwards, Earl, 13
Eller, Carl, 35, 115
Elliot, Bump, 45
Elliot, John, 76
Elzey, Bob, 66
Eysoldt, Vince, 21

Fellowship of Christian Athletes (FCA), 134–35
Fernandez, Manny, 124, 127
Fiss, Galen, 58
Foley, Tim, 124, 135
Forzano, Rick, 23, 25, 28
Fritsch, Toni, 107–8, 149

Gabriel, Roman, 111
Garrison, Walt, 14, 76, 94, 98, 128, 130, 136, 150
Goshawks Pensacola football team. See Pensacola Naval Air Station (Goshawks)
Graham, Otto, 57
Gramblin, Bobby, 51
Grammer, Mike, 62–63
Green, Cornell, 95
Green Bay Packers, 61, 122
Griese, Bob, 106; compared with Roger Staubach, 120–21, 127–28

Hardin, Wayne, 25, 28, 33–41, 44, 46
Harraway, Charlie, 97–98
Harris, Cliff, 99
Hayes, Bob, 10, 67, 94, 99, 108, 111, 114, 116, 127, 133
Hayes, Woody, 24
Heisman Trophy, 25, 28, 49, 57, 113
Henderson, Neil, 40
Hill, Calvin, 10, 13–14, 76, 85, 98, 104, 112–13, 130, 136, 148, 150, 152
Hill, Winston, 135
Holden, Tom, 63
Homan, Dennis, 67, 84
Hoobler, Marianne (Mrs. Roger Staubach), 20, 31, 47, 58–59, 60, 139–41
Hornsby, Ron, 114
Howley, Chuck, 10, 94, 131
Huarte, John, 57
Hunt, Lamar, 58

Jefferson, Roy, 97
Johnson, Curtis, 124
Johnson, Lyndon, President, 101, 126
Jordan, Lee Roy, 10, 12, 94
Jurgensen, Sonny, 82, 92

Kansas City Chiefs, 122
Kennedy, John F., President, 39, 42
Kiick, Jim, 125, 131
Kilmer, Bill, 92, 97, 150
Kirkpatrick, C. C., Rear Admiral, 52
Kleinfeldt, Richard, 22–24
Klemick, Ron, 35–36
Kolen, Mike, 124
Kosciusko, Joe, 44
Kwalick, Ted, 13, 135

Lamonica, Daryle, 135
Landry, Greg, 118, 144, 146
Landry, Tom (Dallas coach), 11, 12, 71, 75–76, 82–87, 103, 115–18, 126, 146–50; Coaching strategy, 68–70; FCA member, 134–36; Policy of calling plays, 109–11; Quarterback rotation, 90–93, 95–100; Super Bowl, 128–31
Larsen, Gary, 115
Lee, Bob, 116–17
Lilly, Bob, 10, 94, 128, 131, 150, 152
Liscio, Tony, 88
Lombardi, Vince, 106
Los Angeles Rams, 69, 91, 111, 152
Lothridge, Billy, 49

McCarthy, Jim, 19–20, 23
McCracken, Tom, 65
McDonald, David L., CNO, U.S. Navy, 50
McKeever, Marlin, 146
Marianne. See Hoobler, Marianne
Marshall, Jim, 115
Mason, Tommy, 98
Mazur, John, 94
Meredith, Don, 67, 71, 74, 82, 93
Merino, Ed, 40
Miami Dolphins, 80, 119–33
Minnesota Vikings, 115–17, 152–53
Mira, George, 49
Momfort, Jerry, 24–25
Morrall, Earl, 82, 92
Morris, Mercury, 127
Morton, Craig, 57–58, 67, 70, 72, 74–75, 77, 90, 93, 96 98–100, 102, 114, 145–48, 151; compared with Staubach, 104; No. 1 quarterback, 86–88
Mosher, Curt, 72, 142

Namath, Joe, 11, 49, 57, 75, 81, 89, 105, 112–13
National Football Conference, 9, 107, 150
National Football League, 9, 12, 56, 105
Naval Academy. See U.S. Naval Academy
Neely, Ralph, 57, 96, 100
New England Patriots, 99, 101–2
New Mexico Military Institute, 26–28, 42

New Orleans Saints, 99–100
New York Giants, 98, 113–14
New York Jets, 57, 112
New York *Times* (quoted), 50
Newsweek, 49
Nitschke, Ray, 135
Nitze, Paul H., Secretary of the Navy, 50
Nixon, Richard, President, 125
NMMI. *See* New Mexico Military Institute
Norman, Pettis, 67
Notre Dame University, 24, 47

O'Bradovich, Ed, 102
O'Brien, Jim, 88
Ohio State (University), 24
Orr, Edward "Skip," 33, 46–47, 52
Osborne, Tom, 134

Page, Alan, 115
Parks, Billy, 148–49
Pearson, Drew, 152
Pensacola Naval Air Station (Goshawks), 63–66
Perkins, Steve, 108, 121
Philadelphia Eagles, 95
Plum, Milt, 92
Pugh, Jethro, 10, 94
Purdue University, 24

Quarterback playing strategy, Pocket theory, 82, 147; Rotating system, 90–91; Shuttle system, 102
Quinn, Joe, 23

Reeves, Dan, 13–14, 96, 136
Renfro, Mel, 10, 128
Rentzel, Lance, 67, 76, 84, 94
Repp, Mike, 64
Rhome, Jerry, 67, 70
Richardson, Gloster, 99
Rickey, Branch, 136
Roesinger, Steve, 60
Rose, Pete, 21
Rosema, Rocky, 85
Royal, Darrell, 50
Ryan, Buddy, 113

Sai, John, 45, 50
Saint Louis Cardinals, 84–87, 106

San Francisco 49ers, 9, 12–15, 88, 117, 148–49
Schramm, Tex, 94, 106
Scott, Jake, 133
Scott, Jim, 124
Sellers, Ron, 149
Sharockman, Ed, 116
Shaw, Bob, 26–27, 42
Shula, Don, 80–81, 120–22, 125
Shy, Les, 85
Simpson, Gary, 65
Snead, Norm, 116
Sport magazine, 132, 140
Stanfill, Bill, 124
Starr, Bart, 61, 105
Staubach, Roger. *See also* Dallas Cowboys
   Awards, 22, 28, 48, 49, 53, 54, 118, 119, 138, 140; Boyhood, 15–18; College football games, 35–38, 45–47, 49–53, 56–58; Compared with Griese, 120–21, with Morton, 103–4; Dallas Cowboys: signs contract, 58–59, No. 1 quarterback, 11, 103, rookie, 72; Injuries, 53, 58, 96, 146–47; Leadership, 12, 21, 27, 104; Marriage and family life, 58, 139–43; Naval Academy, 12, 22–25, 28, 29–56; Navy duty, 12, 56–72; Parents, 15–18, 24, 31, 42, 47–49; Sports: high school, 16, 18–23; NMMI, 26–28; Quarterback techniques, 11, 20, 27, 45, 73, 77, 82–83, 113, 118, 147; Religion, 19, 134–40; Statistics, 41, 48, 54, 55, 113, 118, 132, 151–52; Scholarship offers, 24; Super Bowl, 1972, 119–33, 143
Steward, Jim, 36
Stofa, John, 121
Super Bowl, 9, 15, 88–89, 119–33, 143
Swift, Doug, 125

Talbert, Diron, 151
Tarkenton, Fran, 69, 89, 113, 135, 146
Taylor, Charlie, 150

157

Texas Stadium, 100–1
Texas University Longhorns, 50–52
Thomas, Duane, 10, 14, 93–94, 98, 101, 106, 111, 113–15, 117, 127, 129, 131
Thomas, Ike, 112
Time magazine cover story, 48
Tom, Mel, 96
Truax, Billy, 98, 102, 109–11, 136

Unitas, Johnny, 82, 105
U.S. Naval Academy, 12, 22, 24–25, 28–56

Van Brocklin, Norm, 91

Warfield, Paul, 22, 125, 128
Washington, Gene, 12, 13
Washington Redskins, 97, 107–8, 117, 150–51
Waterfield, Bob, 91
Waters, Charlie, 99, 116
Westmoreland, General William, 43–44
Wilcox, Dave, 14, 148
Wilson, George, 92
Wilson, Larry, 85–86
Wright, Rayfield, 131

Yepremian, Garo, 122, 130

Zone defense, 77–82

The Author

George Sullivan has written a good-sized shelf of books as a free-lance author. Born in Lowell, Massachusetts, he is a graduate of Fordham University. At present he lives in New York with his wife and son, Timothy.